THE
STRENGTH
OF A WOMAN!

*I Love you
Mrs. Johnson*

INGRID CHARLERY

outskirts
press

The Strength of a Woman
Through the Darkness Came Light and Strength
All Rights Reserved.
Copyright © 2019 Ingrid Charlery
v2.0

The opinions expressed in this manuscript are solely the opinions of the author and do not represent the opinions or thoughts of the publisher. The author has represented and warranted full ownership and/or legal right to publish all the materials in this book.

This book may not be reproduced, transmitted, or stored in whole or in part by any means, including graphic, electronic, or mechanical without the express written consent of the publisher except in the case of brief quotations embodied in critical articles and reviews.

Outskirts Press, Inc.
http://www.outskirtspress.com

Paperback ISBN: 978-1-9772-0926-9
Hardback ISBN: 978-1-9772-1000-5

Cover © 2019 Designs By Sam. All rights reserved - used with permission.

Outskirts Press and the "OP" logo are trademarks belonging to Outskirts Press, Inc.

PRINTED IN THE UNITED STATES OF AMERICA

Foreword

THIS IS THE inspirational story of Ingrid Charley, an immigrant from St Lucia Island in the West Indies. The book provides a vivid insight to the life of this young woman and how she survived through the power of prayer against seemingly insurmountable emotional pain. Two catastrophic relationships both characterized by blind love and heartbreaking betrayal drag her from the crest of the happiness wave to the treacherous rocks of broken promises and shattered dreams. The events and experiences of abuse, lies and underhandedness provide the foundation of this heartrending story. Ingrid describes in graphic detail how circumstances forced here and her young daughter from a comfortable home onto dirty floors and uncomfortable beds in shelters for the homeless.

When the true colors of the man she loves emerge, and she discovers she has been living with a psychopathic drug addict she knows she has to escape. But it is not that easy.

On the verge of following in her own parent's footsteps by leaving her daughter in the care of a foster home, Ingrid had planned to go one further and take her own life. Her awakening and new found emotional strength through the power of prayer and the hand of God make this true life drama a spellbinding read..

Today, Ingrid is a public speaker and a counselor for the depressed, desperate and suicidal.

The Strength of A Woman is a true story.

The people, places and experienced related in this book are all real. However where appropriate, the names of individuals, places and institutions have been changed to protect both the author and those who played a part in the life of Ingrid.

Prologue

IT'S 3 A.M. and I can't sleep. My heart is filled to bursting with excitement, my thoughts a fusion of possibilities. For the first time in months, I am happy. I am a survivor,... a winner. I have come through a period in my life that's been a living hell and have emerged stronger and wiser, having wrestled with, and overcome, my greatest adversary, the demon of depression!... Now I'm in control. I'm alive and positive and on the brink of a new dawn for my daughter Samantha and myself.

I see myself rising from victim to victor, a powerful voice with the confidence to believe in myself. To me, failure is no longer an option. The cure for my disease has been positive thought, prayer, and the hand of God. I fought with all I had, through the tears, frustration and humiliation, and reached out for freedom of spirit. Now the sky, with God as my guide, is my limit.

I am free from hearing "no we can't help you", free from being told, "Unfortunately, we don't help individuals, we only help nonprofit organizations, best of luck to you".... Free from being turned away over and over again, free from believing the world has a vendetta against me and an obligation to kick me repeatedly while I'm down. At last we will be free from homelessness, not dependant on shelters. We are heading to a place we can call OUR home.

It is difficult to describe the sense of overwhelming exhilaration and joy one feels when you realise your shackles have come off, that your life is about to change and you are no longer bound by the restrictive dark walls of depression and despair. It's like waking up from a turbulent night of recurrent nightmares, relieved you don't have to revisit them and looking out on the dawn of a new day with clear blue skies and bright sunshine over fields of wide open spaces and colourful flowers. Love for life bubbles from within and I make a pledge to myself:

> *From today I will help others. I will help those in need of an understanding ear and a shoulder to offload on. I will care for those suffering from depression and help them stay focused by speaking, encouraging and guiding them through prayer and God's mercy.*

It's March 30th 2017, I'm in my narrow bed in my room at 17 Kent Place, Summit New Jersey, a shelter for the homeless. I'm feeling so good about myself and my new found hope but I'm reminded of where I've been. My thoughts drift back over the months gone by. Frustrating, daunting months during which life had turned on me and been unbearably cruel. I'm reminded with a sense of horror, of the days when I had believed my only way out was to abandon my precious daughter to child care where she would be looked after, then take my own life. The inspiration to take such drastic action had been real. The depth of my despair had clouded my sanity, and the angel of death had gestured like a phantom of peaceful escape, enticing me towards the comforting darkness of final oblivion and welcome release. The temptation to follow that ghostly instinct had, at times, been overwhelming

For the thousandth time, I piece together the events of my life, events that took me from a free spirited soul, working in a job I loved, sharing my life with a man I thought I loved and having the time and freedom to take trips to Canada and to my family home on St. Lucia in the Caribbean. How had I allowed my life to change so dramatically, how had my spirit been so spectacularly ripped apart and left in tatters on the dirty floors or uncomfortable beds of inhospitable shelters for the homeless?

Chapter 1

THE TROPICAL ISLAND of St. Lucia is a small West Indian nation in the east Caribbean. There are not many places on planet earth to compare with its rare unblemished beauty. The spirit of the island rubs off on those who live there and its splendor remains forever embellished in the minds of those who visit. It's an island of volcanic peaks and virgin jungle, surrounded by sapphire blue, crystal clear ocean waters. Scuba diving, snorkeling, water skiing, tree-top zip line adventures, game fishing, bustling markets and a vibrant nightlife epitomize the island's lifestyle. Very few of the native islanders are rich in the traditional sense; however the richness of life makes the possession of material wealth inconsequential and superfluous.

I grew up in a foster home on the island. My 'Mom' had taken me in when my parents had been proven incapable of caring for me as a baby. Mom gave me a stable upbringing, filled with love, joy and high moral values. She was a strict God fearing woman with fourteen children of her own, and I was taken in and grew up with them like a real sibling. Mom gave us all everything any child could wish for and my young life was one embodied in tranquility, infectious laughter and an untroubled existence.

St. Lucia's economy is almost entirely dependent on

tourism and the export of bananas. Consequently unless one has a calling to work a banana plantation, wait tables, open a restaurant or find work in a hotel, career opportunities are in short supply. Young people with ambition mostly leave the island to study or find work in the United States once their secondary schooling is complete. I was no exception. My dream was to become a nurse and shortly after my eighteenth birthday, I bade an emotional farewell to my family and boarded an aircraft at Hewanorra International Airport en route to America in search of a way to make my career aspirations a reality.

I was fortunate to have an aunt in New Jersey, and I settled in with her initially, but the lack of transport, and consequent inability to get around trying to find work to pay for my studies was holding me back. I needed to move to where there was public transport and more employment opportunities, and after a few weeks I boarded a train from Orange New Jersey and headed for New York. A childhood friend, Sara, living in Brooklyn made space for me in her tiny apartment while I looked for a job

Moving from the islands to New York as a naïve teenager, is a culture shock they have not yet invented words to describe. To say it terrified me is an understatement of epic proportions. To say it intrigued me and absorbed me despite my trepidation sounds like a contradiction of terms. Yet somehow, between fear, fascination, and watching Sara, I gradually slipped into a comfort zone amid the hustle and bustle of America's biggest and busiest city. Two weeks after my arrival, I was offered a job as a live in nanny Mondays to Fridays in Roselyn Long Island, which gave me time to explore over weekends or go to my aunt in New Jersey.

CHAPTER 1

Having Sara's helping hand was a blessing. She had been there long enough to feel at home in the city and her confidence rubbed off on me. She showed me the shops and the nightlife and took me with her to social gatherings. I was soon familiar with the city's transport system and able to come and go without thinking I would get lost and sucked up into the belly of New York, never to be seen again.

That all happened fifteen years ago and time has moved on. I gave up the nanny job in Long Island to go back to New Jersey where I could attend a school for nurses. During that time a friend introduced me to Peter, Samantha's father. Peter had lived in New Jersey all his life and he was great company. He taught me to drive and encouraged me in my studies and eventually helped me get a position as a therapist's assistant at Hamilton Family Park, a nursing home close to where I lived in Elizabeth. As our relationship blossomed and we became lovers, Peter played a major part in my life. He was exciting to be with, we had much in common but most of all we enjoyed each other. After almost a year of being together and stealing time whenever we could, making wild passionate love secretly, we found a place of our own and moved in together.

When I was 24, I got pregnant with Samantha and life changed. I had gone back to school part time to complete my nursing degree, and the unexpected pregnancy complicated our lives in ways we would never have thought possible. Trying to juggle the balls of being a student with a full time job is bad enough, but trying to be a good full time mom on top of it became too much of a challenge and Peter said it wasn't right. He wanted me to give more time to our baby, but we couldn't afford our expenses on only one income so I left college but carried on working mornings. Samantha was looked after at a nearby daycare center.

Peter and I had been living together for 6 years when Samantha was born and we'd been happy. We'd never married, but chose to get married after the birth. We had been together whenever we weren't working. We had travelled to many places together and he loved coming home with me to St. Lucia. We delighted in the beauty of snorkeling and scuba diving, particularly off Pigeon Point where the coral and fish varieties are especially colourful. Those had been exhilarating experiences and we never tired of exploring the beauty of the reefs. We were the perfect couple. We were in love and it was an unspoken foregone conclusion we'd be together forever. But then something changed.

It's hard to define exactly what changed or when the mold started to creep in, but it gradually permeated our relationship like an odour. For no apparent reason we seemed to drift apart and become an irritation to each other. We argued over irrelevant subjects, something we had never done before. What had once been rapturous passion in our love making deteriorated to a kind of meaningless clinical activity, like an art form of masturbation. Peter started working late more often and on far too many occasions I was already in bed by the time he got home.

When Samantha turned four, we planned a special birthday party for her. All the children from her play group were invited and it should have been a splendid event, but

CHAPTER 1

Peter didn't show up. He had said he would be home early to join in the festivities, but he just never showed up. I had cleared away and put Samantha to bed by the time he came home and I was furious. That night, we had the most vicious fight we had ever had, and every unspoken, papered over flaw in our ten year relationship was laid bare. We were on a mission to see who could hurt the other more deeply. And then my world fell apart. Peter blurted out to me that he had been seeing another woman for over a year.

The term *"crushed"* forms a dismally inadequate description for the blow his words delivered. It was like a roundhouse punch from a professional boxer hitting me squarely against the head, shaking the senses and blurring the vision. I stood looking at him, trying to convince myself it wasn't true, I'd misheard him, trying to believe it was a bad dream from which I would awaken, but I knew I was deceiving myself. I stood staring at him for what seemed like a long time, and there was total silence, as if all sound in the world around us had suddenly been muted. Finally, without a word, I turned away and went to our bedroom. I closed and locked the door and threw myself onto the bed where I remained, desolate and sobbing inconsolably until, many hours later, I fell into a fitful sleep. Life as I knew it had come to an abrupt end.

When I rose, Peter was still there. He had slept on the sofa in the lounge, but looked ruffled and bleary eyed, as though his night's sleep had been as disruptive as mine.

"I can't stay with you Peter." I was holding back fresh tears and struggling to keep my voice steady. "You have destroyed me, you have broken my heart and I will never be able to forgive you. I have to have a place for Samantha, so I'm staying here until that is taken care of, but I want you out."

"Where do you suppose I'll go?" His expression was challenging, almost arrogant and I had to hold myself back from slapping him or spitting in his face.

I exploded. "Go to your fucking mistress, go to hell, I really don't care, just get out of this house. I never want to see you again,"

Samantha had not come out of her room and I was hoping she was still asleep. I didn't want her to witness the anger and bitterness that had grown like a virus overnight. I would try to explain to her later. Right at that moment, I just wanted to be left alone and I wanted this man who had been an extension of myself for ten years, the man I had loved unconditionally, to be gone from my life. I had no idea what I was going to do, it was as if I had been sucked into a vacuum and was floating helplessly, desperately trying to find something solid to hold onto. For the first time in my life, the term 'heartbroken' had a meaning I truly understood.

Chapter 2

HOW DOES ONE define a broken heart? There is no snapping of bone, no crushing of vertebrae, no torn skin or bleeding wounds, no outward appearance of physical pain or bodily damage... NO!! Heartbreak is a very personal, very lonely internalized state of mind and it is infinitely more painful than the breaking of bones.

In my case it was characterized by a sense of betrayal, a disturbing upheaval of emotional turmoil, like a kaleidoscope of grief and anger, hatred and love, blame and guilt. Painful waves of confusion, swirling around within me... Self destructive mood swings and irrational thoughts of revenge permeated my core, and the constant burden of self pity clutched at my heart like a clamp. The only thing that kept me sane was my unwavering dedication to Samantha's wellbeing, and through the pain and depression, I clung to that as a drowning woman would cling to a buoy.

I had been so completely unprepared for Peter's revelation; the circumstances I had to face were so foreign, I had no idea where to turn. The word *'divorce'* stuck in my throat like a tumor, but I had to find the strength to straighten out my life and move forward alone.

At first getting through a day, trying to cope with the internal conflict of self worth challenged me. Trying not to let my devastation rub off on Samantha was like trying not to fall when losing your footing. Then a week had gone by and the void in my life seemed to widen. I felt as though time stood still, spitefully tormenting me, dragging out each hour of emotional agony, making it more difficult for me to cope before finally allowing me a few hours of respite, grudgingly granted by troubled sleep. Something deep inside of me had died and I grieved its passing with all the sorrow one feels at the death of a loved one.

My colleagues at Trinitas Hospital, where I had worked as a medical receptionist and translator since before Samantha was born, treated me with compassion afforded to a grieving widow. Their kindness helped me through those difficult weeks and very slowly I started to heal. My fits of depression and anxiety gradually diminished and the torment in my soul was replaced by something else. It was as if my entire being had been drained of an essential element, leaving me wasted and desolate but now it was progressively being replenished with stronger stuff, raising me from a deep black hole of despair back to ground level and a resemblance of who I had once been. Through the anguish of my life imploding, I had kept a roof over our heads and been able to put food on the table and I counted that as an achievement.

The divorce was a messy affair. Peter insisted through his attorney that I had been the catalyst for him to stray from our relationship. His plea had been that it had been me who had been guilty of infidelity long before he had met the woman he had been sleeping with. He changed jobs in a bizarre move to hide his income so he didn't have to pay alimony, and he got away with the minimum of child support. It was the most demoralizing revelation to discover

CHAPTER 2

what a sham our relationship had been. Listening to the lies contained in the arguments and the bargaining on the subject of what my fate would be, was like the detachment of watching a heart rending movie with characters and actors I neither knew nor had ever heard of before, but who's lines would have a direct and profound effect on my existence. The dishonesty was obscene, and as we moved through the process of our legal separation the sense that I had ever loved this man repulsed me. I'd been with him for ten years and I didn't even know him. Now I hated him.

The settlement finally reached after months of excruciating court appearances and legal wrangling, resulted in me retaining custody of Samantha with visitation rights for Peter. Every second weekend he would be allowed to pick up Samantha on a Friday after work and bring her back to me on Sunday evening. He was ordered to pay $ 100.00 per month towards child support. It would have suited me better if he had kept his child support check and got out of our lives far away and forever. The idea that I would have to see him at all filled me with a fervor resembling repugnance.

I needed to improve my income. Samantha's child support was barely enough to cover the daycare center, and she was growing out of her clothes almost before we got her home from the store we'd bought them in. My training qualified me as a daycare nurse and there were private jobs being advertised in wealthy areas where parents could afford to have their children looked after by a full time nanny. Those jobs paid far better than the reception job I had at Trinitas and although I was happy there and reluctant to leave, I needed the extra money. Three months after the divorce was final I signed up with an agency.

Most of the jobs were short term assignments, usually for periods of a month or less while parents were away travelling or attending to commitments of business. Occasionally an assignment as a parent's assistant would come up and I'd be on hand to help aloof mothers who found diaper changing repugnant or who felt being a mother was an intrusion on their social life. Jobs like that could last up to six months or more and would normally be shared in shifts with a night nurse. Being a baby lover, I found the work inspiring and as time moved on I adapted to life as a single parent.

One of the benefits of agency work was the ability to take time off between assignments. I would try to time those gaps to coincide with Samantha's school breaks, and we'd take off for a few days to different parts of the country or to Toronto, a city I loved and where my cousin Alana and her husband Sherwin lived.

Samantha and I had moved out of the house we'd lived in with Peter and found a cute, affordable two bedroom apartment in Springfield. It was close to her school and walking distance to busses and trains.

I had been with the agency for nearly three years when they referred me to a full time employer, Kate & Barry Howard, who would pay me independently. There were four children, the oldest of which was 6 and the youngest just 2 months. It was a "direct employment" contract through the permanent employment division of the agency. The money was better than the weekly wage I had received from the agency and there was no agency fee deduction. The address was really up market New Jersey. My enthusiasm to work on a direct basis would have consequences I had never anticipated or considered.

CHAPTER 2

I shared duties with a German immigrant named Irina, who was a full time live in au pair.

Bill was the oldest child at 6, then James who was 3, Lilly coming up 2 and baby Jean.

I came to adore the children I cared for almost as much as my own cherished daughter. During the day while I was there, Irina gave most of her attention to Bill. He would reach school going age the following year and she was teaching him the basics of reading, writing and counting.

My day would start by getting my charges bathed and dressed, and feeding them their breakfast. I took care of the younger three. Lilly loved dishing out wet baby kisses and I never discouraged it. James loved to be chased around the garden, and I managed to balance my attention between them. Jean still slept most of the time, waking only to be fed, winded and changed, although there were times when she was a real handful and niggled and cried for no reason I could identify.

I made a point of encouraging laughter and contentment. Happy children are so responsive and I used every bit of child psychology I knew, to keep their little spirits alert and satisfied. On days when the weather was warm and dry, we'd take the stroller and walk in a nearby park, I read to them and we sang songs together. Irina and Bill occasionally joined us but the age gap between him and the others was too great to keep his attention for very long and Irina would go off and occupy him with more advanced activities.

I liked Irina and we got on well together. She was a devout Christian and during quiet periods when the children were napping and we went about our chores doing laundry, preparing their meals or sterilizing bottles and teats, we would have long conversations about her faith. She wasn't bothered by the fact that I had a resistance towards religion. I had grown up in a foster home with a wonderfully loving 'Mom.' She was a strict, God fearing woman who zealously believed in the Bible. We were forced to go to church on Saturdays where the preacher would shower down upon us promises of fire and brimstone with a violent fiery hell for sinners,

"You are ALL sinners." He would bellow from the pulpit waving a pointed finger high above his head. We would ALL be sent there by God who, we were told, loved us. That didn't make a lot of sense to me and as I grew up, and realized the advantage of independent thought, I found myself disregarding religious instruction as being just a little bit inconsistent with reality. Paying attention to my eternal salvation had not been a priority for me since leaving St. Lucia.

Caring for those children gave me a sense of satisfaction and fulfillment. I would never let it extend to a point where Samantha was neglected or even came second, but I loved my job. I was content, and although thoughts of Peter, and the happier times we had spent together, frequently appeared in my thoughts, I was over the torment of our break up and had found contentment. Kate and Barry clearly considered the choice of nanny for their offspring to have been a good one. On the infrequent occasions they participated in daily activities with me and the children, there were always complimentary and encouraging words for me and I appreciated their kindness.

One morning while heading down the stairs from the nursery, Jean in my arms and Lilly two paces behind skipping along happily, I lost my footing and slipped on the stairway. My first concern was for the baby and I grabbed out frantically for the railing with my left hand while subconsciously and in slow motion, planning how I was going to break my fall without dropping the child. As it happened, the railing saved us and I regained my balance but I had caught my foot between the balustrade and a step, twisting it so the pain shot up through my leg and made a charged attempt at blasting its way through the top of my head. Tears came to my eyes as I tried to suppress a scream of sheer agony. Irina had been behind Lilly with Bill and James in tow and she relieved me of Jean while I hobbled down the rest of the flight to find somewhere to sit.

For the rest of that day I felt nauseous with the pain. My right foot felt as though it had been the victim of a hammer wielding brute, who had landed a vicious, unimpeded blow squarely against the knuckle behind my big toe, I had never known such pain. I knew I had done some serious damage and would need to have it attended to.

I called and made an appointment to see my doctor on my way home that evening. I couldn't drive and had to take a cab, collecting Samantha from school along the way. My foot had swollen to an abnormal size and I had been unable to keep my shoes on. Putting weight on the foot was impossible and the agony didn't subside for a moment.

"You've bruised yourself pretty badly." The doctor prodded gently, almost sending me up through the roof from the torture of her touch. "It seems you've whacked it in the region of the navicular bone. The extent of the damage will only show up under an X-ray, but that foot is far too swollen to get a decent picture. For now, the best I can do is strap it and prescribe pain killers and an anti inflammatory. We'll look at again once the swelling goes down."

She gave me an injection containing a cocktail of comfort drugs and two bottles of pills with written instructions on dosage and frequency of administration. I left the rooms on crutches, very worried about how I could do my job while incapacitated in that way. I would just have to toughen up.

The discomfort persisted for days, although the severity of the pain and the swelling subsided under the influence of the pills. Irina was fantastic and went the extra mile to help with my duties as well as taking care of her own. Kate and Barry were incredibly understanding and sympathetic. They offered to get a part time nurse to stand in for me if needed. That was the last thing I wanted, so I gritted my teeth and did the best I could.

When I returned to have the foot X-rayed, I got the news I hadn't wanted to hear.

"You have what is known as *extra accessory navicular syndrome*." The doctor informed me. "That's an extra bit of bone or piece of cartilage attached to the navicular. It shouldn't be there. It's a congenital condition and you would probably never have been aware of it had you not had the accident with the stairs. You're going to need surgery to remove it. Basically, we make an incision and cut away the offending bone. It's really quick and the recovery period is not much more than two weeks, maybe three."

I was horrified. That meant I would have to take leave and I had planned to use my leave to go home to St. Lucia. If I was to have the surgery it meant being off for three weeks and that was the extent of the leave I was due. I decided to see if I could dodge the surgery. My foot was getting better and although still tender, I could walk on it and it was improving all the time. Maybe surgery was a bit of overkill. Two weeks after the first incident, while playing a tag game with James, I twisted the foot again and ended up back on the crutches. I knew then that surgery was inevitable. When I confirmed with my doctor I would go ahead, I was told it could not be done until September. We were only in June so it would be almost three months and I had planned to go to St. Lucia in August. The timing was so bad and it really annoyed me, but there was nothing I could do about it.

Chapter 3

OVER THE MONTHS and years following our divorce, Peter and I had gotten beyond our differences. The heartbreak he had inflicted on me had slowly diminished and healed, allowing our association to settle into a cordial but non-committal sort of coalition. The one thing we still had in common was the love for our child and time had forced us into an agreeable truce.

On the weekends Samantha spent with him, I frequently joined friends after work on the Friday for drinks and dinner at the Don Felix. It was a diner style restaurant and bar on Elizabeth Avenue and the food was excellent. One Friday, a regular member of our group was with her cousin, a great looking guy who she introduced as Rob.

It was the most extraordinary experience. Rob and I seemed to be drawn to each other as if destiny had brought us to this place to renew a bond from a previous life or another dimension. From the moment we were introduced a feeling of camaraderie settled between us, a mysterious awareness of déjà vu. It felt as though we'd been here before, like opening the door into a place not visited in a long time, but immediately recognizing it and feeling at home there. We chatted amiably among the company, but kept being drawn back to conversation with each other. There was an unspoken expectation that this chance meeting would lead to something more, and I was neither surprised nor hesitant when he asked me to meet him for lunch on the Sunday. As I was alone for the weekend, it seemed a great opportunity to get out and get to know this alluring stranger better.

Rob and I blended like sunshine in a gentle breeze. We laughed easily together, discovered we had the same taste in movie entertainment and enjoyed the same food. He listened intently as I told him about St. Lucia, my childhood, my family at home and about Samantha and my marriage to Peter. I told him of the work I did caring for children. He told me of his broken marriage and his son Christopher. He spoke of his family and his enthusiasm for his career and the company he worked for. The afternoon sped by amid relaxed conversation and easy laughter. Time seemed to evaporate, and we were both surprised when we suddenly became aware it was dark outside and I had to get home to be there when Peter dropped Samantha. We parted at my car, where he planted a polite peck on both my cheeks and thanked me for a wonderful afternoon. As I drove away, I experienced mixed sensation of joy and exhilaration as though I had been intoxicated by spiritual fizz. The feeling made me want to dance and burst into song. I knew I liked this guy a lot. He had opened up and filled something inside of me that had been neglected and left dormant for far too long. I couldn't wait to hear from him again.

I didn't have long to wait, I had no sooner walked into my apartment when my mobile phone rang. "Unknown Caller" I read on the screen. I was in two minds to take the call or cancel it but chose to answer.

"I cannot remember a day when I enjoyed myself so

much" It was Rob's voice

I laughed delightedly. "Strange you should say that. I'm trying to remember when last I was in the company of someone so easy to be with"

"When can we do it again?" there was a smile in his voice and I could picture the grin on his face.

"Not until next weekend at the earliest. I have bills to pay, a daughter to care for and a job that makes it all possible"

"Would you spend next weekend with me if I asked you?"

"Would you allow me to bring my daughter as a chaperone?"

"Only if I can bring my son as a distraction for the chaperone"

"I may have to clear that with the chaperone."

He laughed at that, and the contentment in his laughter had contagious joy in it.

"If I phone you every day this week, would you think I was coming on to you?" There was a mischievous tilt in his voice.

"If you don't phone me every day this week, I'll think you're rude." I taunted. This was starting to sound like telephonic foreplay. We were consciously coming on to each other. I figured it was time to cut. "My ex has just arrived with Samantha" I lied. "Got to go. Have a wonderful week and don't forget to call." We said good bye and cut the call.

The work week seemed to take forever to go by. Rob called every evening, and I sat on the sofa with my legs curled up under my rump as we chatted. Our calls went on for ages and covered subjects about everything in general and nothing in particular. It was effortless, familiar banter interspersed with good-natured teasing and spontaneous laughter. I found myself eagerly looking forward to his calls and the upcoming weekend. But I was also plagued by indecision. In the wake of my break up with Peter, my interest in men or any kind of relationship with one was non-existent. After we split up my libido had to retreated into a psychologically protected box marked 'celibate.' I'd simply had no interest in sex or men. Now, Rob had broken into that box of locked away yearning, and the contents had spilled out with a flourish, urgently demanding attention. In spite of my sudden revival and the emergence of an almost forgotten, smoldering sensation of lust, I felt the need to nurture what was developing between us. I was cautiously excited by this unexpected romance, but I didn't want to rush things. Added to my caution was the impressionable Samantha. She was coming on ten, and a constant sponge of natural curiosity. Creating a new source for her to ponder didn't seem like a great idea. When Rob called on the Friday night, I subtly let it be known we would not be sharing sleeping quarters over the weekend. He seemed neither fazed nor offended and it was evident the approach to our emerging destiny was being handled with mutual forethought and caution. Life seemed to have morphed from winter to spring, bursting into bloom, and I was willingly being intoxicated by its pollens. It felt marvelous.

The weekend worked out pretty much as planned, Rob arrived to fetch us on the Saturday morning and we went to the beach. Samantha and Christopher, who at first seemed a bit wary of each other, soon got over their inhibitions and found common ground. The whole day was naturally fun filled. It was the kind of day they write about in romance novels with lots of laughter and walks in the surf holding hands, throwing a ball and eating ice cream from the cone. We went to a beach side diner for an early dinner then back to my apartment where we bathed and fed the exhausted children and put them down to sleep in Samantha's room.

We could so easily have ended up making love that night, but we didn't. We shared deep passionate kisses and held each other close, bordering on getting our clothes off but we both held back. We wanted each other so badly, but it wasn't the right time or place, particularly with the children in the room next to the lounge where our mutual lust filled torment was happening. We both knew the time would come and I think we both wanted it to be perfect in every way when it did. Eventually Rob said he should go, and he collected Christopher and carried him sleeping to his car. Christopher would have to go back to his mother the following day, his weekend with his father over until the following month. We kissed deeply when saying good bye and the taste lingered long after I had returned to the apartment. It had been a long time since I had experienced a state of such complete wellbeing and I started to think about asking Rob to come with me to St.Lucia.

Samantha was going to summer camp and I had planned to go to the island while she was away. The needed surgery to my foot was holding me back, and I wondered if I could take unpaid leave from Kate and Barry so as to do both. I resolved to ask them first thing on Monday before bringing it up with Rob.

Chapter 4

IT WAS A glorious Monday morning. Not a cloud in the sky, and an embracing sense of well being in my heart. The beautiful bright summer sunshine made me think of the beach and to match my mood, I wore my favorite blue and white top. I looked good and felt great. My thoughts drifted to the sandy beaches and sapphire blue seas of St Lucia.

I had worked out arrangements with Kate and Barry and they had been more than accommodating, saying I could take sick leave for the surgery without compromising my annual leave. They would hire a stand in nurse. I was so grateful, I'd leapt up and hugged them both and they laughed at my excitement.

Once having received their blessing, I had shared my thoughts with Rob and he loved the idea of coming home with me to meet my family and visit the places where I'd grown up. We had set about planning the trip together, and this was the beginning of my final week at work. We were due to leave on the morning of the upcoming Saturday

The excitement was so intense I couldn't sleep. Ever since we had agreed on the plans for the trip I had been preoccupied with concern over what Rob would think about St. Lucia. He'd never been to the Caribbean before. I Googled the Island to show him pictures of the beautiful beaches, so much more picturesque than those on the East Coast around New Jersey. We did a virtual tour of the zip-line adventure and watched a video about snorkeling and diving around the coral reefs. I told him I would take him diving and teach him to snorkel. There was so much I wanted to show him and share with him and he seemed to be as excited and enthusiastic about the trip as I was.

Still, I was nervous. I wanted the vacation to go off without a hitch and for Rob to thoroughly enjoy himself. I wanted him to like everything about me, including my roots and my family. I wanted him to experience and appreciate real Caribbean beaches and the beauty of the jungle and craggy volcanic peaks. I wanted him to taste the organic fruits and vegetables from the plants right in our own back yard. I was going to give him the treat of a lifetime with real island hospitality.

The week went by in a blur of busy children and of showing my substitute the ropes of our routine. By the time Friday afternoon came, I was exhausted but satisfied my absence of 4 weeks would not disrupt the children's normal schedule. As I kissed them good bye, I felt a wrench in my heart realizing how much I was going to miss them.

The next morning we were in superbly high spirits. I had dropped Samantha off with Peter the previous evening and he was going to see her off to summer camp. Rob and I were holding hands in the back of a cab on our way to JFK Airport for our flight to St Lucia. I was thrilled that this man, who I was falling in love with, was coming with me and would meet my family and friends in the land of my birth. I turned to Rob and we kissed softly, and I could taste his toothpaste and mouthwash.

We had become lovers in my bed the weekend after our beach day with the children six weeks previously. Samantha had gone to Peter for the weekend and Christopher was with his mother. Rob and I went out for a light dinner and then back to my apartment to watch a movie on television. Well, that was never going to work. The moment we were alone in the apartment, all the frustration of wanting each other and holding back, all the pent up passion of lust we had bottled up inside of ourselves exploded like a bursting dam and we molested each other with an intensity bordering on obsession. The experience was like entering a 4th dimension; an out of body journey into paradise and we couldn't get enough of each other. It had been so long since I had made love and I was quite sure I had never experienced anything as intensely fulfilling as that first encounter with Rob. We'd spent the night together and lost count of how many times we went back for more.

The next morning, Rob asked me to give up my apartment and move in with him.

"My place is big enough for us. I have two bedrooms and a loft. Samantha will have her own room bigger than the cubicle she has now."

He was trying so hard to sell the idea to me, and it did not take much persuasion. I felt so totally in tune with this man, I didn't think it was right for us to be apart. Samantha and I had moved out of our apartment and settled into our new home with Rob ten days later.

Now it felt wonderful being with him on our way to meet my family in the place I had grown up. I was so excited about our trip. I was eager for him to meet the people

I'd told him so much about and for him to encounter the warm, clear atmosphere and hospitality of St. Lucia where the sun and the breeze feels good against the skin.

At the airport, he was attentive and opened the door to the cab for me. It was so good to be with this warm, considerate man who cared for me and who practiced old fashion values, like opening doors for his woman.

We made our way through the noisy terminal to the Mac Donald's to get breakfast. We each ordered a Big Mac meal and sat close while we waited for it.

"Do you think she'll like me?" asked Rob.

"Who, mom?...She'll adore you, just like I do." I replied laughing. "She's the most wonderful woman in the whole world and she loves everyone."

The bond between Mom and I was as enduring as if we were biologically related. The love we shared came from deep within us. She had brought me up as part of her large family, and taught us to stay together no matter what. People were important to her.

"I still can't help being nervous." Rob smiled ruefully. "It's not easy being a guest of someone you've never met. Especially when you're sleeping with her daughter."

I sat on his lap and put an arm around his neck with a finger to his nose smiling down at him. "Don't worry about it. It's going to be fine."

As I took my finger away, I noticed a blemish at the corner of his mouth, like a fever blister erupting. I looked closer and touched it saying "Oh dear… too much kissing. We'll have to slow down."

I was unprepared for his reaction. Almost as if it he was swatting a fly, he pushed my hand away and looked annoyed. He put a finger to the spot and looked embarrassed.

"Hey," I said with a bright smile. "It's just a little blemish. Don't look so upset."

"Sorry" his tone was sharp, "I hate little blemishes." Then he relaxed and smiled again. But his reaction had startled me. It was the first time I'd seen him annoyed, and over something so trivial. I soon let it pass and forgot all about it but I would have good reason to remember it again about two months later.

Chapter 5

THE CABIN CREW on the JetBlue flight directed us to our seats and we fastened our lap straps. I held Rob's hand and it felt warm and strong in mine. As we started to roll along the runway picking up speed, I turned to him. "You ready for this?"

"I am." He said. He leaned across to kiss me and squeezed my hand. As the wheels left the tarmac, he picked up the sports magazine he'd brought along for the flight and settled down to read it. I watched the in flight movie for a while, but it wasn't very good so I turned it off and struck up a conversation with the lady in the seat next to me.

She was a widow on a world tour and informed me she was there to ski. I looked at her quizzically. Water skiing was one of the highlights of St. Lucia, but she was a most unlikely looking candidate for such an activity. "I would never have imagined you on a pair of skis" I said politely.

"Depends on how you look at it my dear," she replied with a wicked grin. "In my case I see it as an acronym as well as a sport. 'Spending Kid's Inheritance.'" It took me a moment to get her drift, and then laughed delightedly when I caught on. We settled into an easy conversation.

She introduced herself as Mabel Barker. She'd never been to the Caribbean before and had chosen St. Lucia randomly by closing her eyes and putting her finger down on a map. Her first three tries had landed her in the Atlantic Ocean but on her fourth try St. Lucia was pinned, so here she was. I was able to make loads of suggestions about where to go, what tours to take and where to eat.

"It's really a beautiful place" I told her. "You're going to love it."

It's a four and a half hour flight from JFK to St. Lucia and we talked non-stop. She was a truly interesting person with a great sense of humor and a mischievous glint in her eye, giving the appearance of someone perpetually amused.

As we completed our final approach to Hewanorra International Airport and the wheels made contact with the runway, I leaned across to Rob and kissed him. "Welcome to the Caribbean" I whispered. "My home"

He fixed me with his irresistible smile and said "Thank you for bringing me here"

As the plane came to a halt at the terminal building and we reached up to retrieve our hand luggage I said farewell to Mabel. I was sorry we wouldn't see each other again. I'd enjoyed her company immensely and I told her so.

Being a native to the island has its advantages. I knew just about everyone who lived there and had sent an email to Aline, an old school friend. She had joined the island police when she left school, and worked in the immigration section. She was waiting for us on the apron when we left the plane and we were given VIP treatment. Whisked into a red room, through passport control and customs, and we were in the terminal meet and greet arrivals hall before a lot of our fellow travelers had disembarked from the aircraft.

The rental car we'd booked through the airline was waiting for us at the curb outside the terminal and I could see Rob was visibly impressed by the smoothness of our arrival and the friendliness and efficiency of the people.

"I could get used to living in a place like this" he said as he loaded our bags into the trunk. "It has such a happy atmosphere. Even the sun seems to shine with a smile."

"You've not seen nothin' yet," I told him with a chuckle, feeling a rush of joy at being home. "This is just the doorway to paradise."

As we left the airport we could smell the blossoms and feel the humid heat typical of the island. It was a beautifully clear day and a fresh breeze blew in through the open car windows diminishing the oppressive effect of 86 degrees outside. It felt so good to be back.

The MicoudHighway is carved through the lush island greenery for almost the entire length of St. Lucia. From the airport to my home town of La-point Mon-Repos it's twenty two kilometers of meandering roadway with dense foliage most of the way on either side. It's a beautiful drive and we could smell the ocean where the road came out of the jungle to run along the coast line, exposing white sandy beaches, starkly contrasted against the clear blue sea.

We drove straight to mom's house and were enthralled by all the friends and family members who had gathered to greet us. There were hugs and kisses and laughter all round and everyone seemed to talk at once as old friendships and family ties were renewed. It was a new experience for Rob, but everyone went out of their way to make him feel part of the family. Once the introductions and the excitement of our arrival had subsided, we were led into the house to be greeted by a prepared feast of St Lucia's best food. Everybody had brought a dish of traditional island fare, prepared to perfection. There were a variety of cooked fish dishes, ground provision and vegetables just the way I liked them – it was like nothing I could get in the US. The way this food was prepared provided flavor on top of flavor. Everyone knew it was Rob's first time in St. Lucia so they had made sure not to disappoint him. He got stuck in, sampling everything, savouring every mouthful and constantly muttering his appreciation. Rob had been impressed by St. Lucia the minute we stepped off the plane, his first meal and the wonderful people around us made him fall in love with the place. The addition of Piton beer consummated his love and made him never want to leave. And we had only just arrived.

Rob was enchanted by mom and charmed her with his wit and easy manner and they quickly fell into effortless conversation. She wanted to know everything about him. What he did and where he had grown up and who his parents were. She fired questions at him, keen to get as much information as quickly as she could. She looked so happy to have us all around her.

After the wonderful lunch, furniture was moved and the music turned up so the dancing could start. I stood up and held out my hand to Rob. "Let's dance."

Dancing is a big part of family, and we all danced for a magical time where nothing could harm us. My parents abandoning me as a baby had long been forgotten.

CHAPTER 5

Knowing I was raised by mom from a very young age and she had done everything a real mom would have done for me made me happy. The fact it hadn't worked out with Samantha's father was forgotten. All the bad experiences I'd had as a child and my broken marriage were put behind me. Everything mom had said 'no' to had been for a good reason, and I'd long ago came to realize that life had been tough for her, but she'd done her best, and then some. Life was as it should be now. It was great, I was happy I had a mother that didn't birth me but loved me unconditionally and a man who I admired more as each day went by. The dancing filled our spirits with love and companionship.

I often told myself you don't have to give birth to a child to be a mother; being a mother comes from the heart. She made me smile and made my heart melt as well. I was happy for all the lessons she taught me and was proud her influence had made me aware of my responsibilities. My life was great, mom had brought us up in a loving Christian home. I had a big family and a loving mother. She was my world and I adored her. I never wanted to even think about letting her down or disappointing her. She had taught me, no matter what, I should always forgive others, be kind and share. As a God fearing woman, she had taught us that we could depend on God for happiness. "People will fail you" she would say. "God will not."

At that time I had my doubts about God and how much he could do for me. Leaving home, I had kind of left God behind to look after the others. He was a bit like a casual acquaintance who came and went without playing a significant role in my life.

Chapter 6

OUR HOLIDAY HAD begun. The family gathering had been the start and couldn't have been a better way to introduce Rob to all the wonderful people I had told him so much about. He was thrilled by the way everyone hugged and kissed their greetings, so full of smiles and laughter. There was so much I wanted to show him, and we only had 10 days.

As everyone had descended on Mom, she had arranged that Rob and I sleep at my dear friend and neighbor Sofia. We had been friends since we were babies and her home was as familiar to me as mom's.

Time seemed to accelerate as each day went by and we threw caution to the wind, energetically filling our days with wonderful activities and loving every moment. We swam in the warm sulphur springs and took a mud bath in the bowl of the world's only "drive in volcano" near beautiful Soufrière. We hired SCUBA gear and went diving off Pigeon Point, where the ocean is crystal clear and the fish life scouring the reef is a constant blaze of colour, just two or three meters below the surface. We strolled hand in hand through the beautiful Botanical Gardens with its exotic plants, and visited Dennery View, from where the island's beauty is in the palm of your hand. Our days were packed, socializing with old friends and taking in the beauty of my homeland. We made a point of enjoying the multitude of facilities offered on the island, to which tourists flock every year. We drove up the coast to Rodney Bay and reveled in the atmosphere of the casinos and the nightlife that goes with it. Our laughter was infectious and we made love whenever we were alone, stealing even the slightest chance to hold each other close. We became immersed in the excitement of each day as we enjoyed the carefree sense of heavenly freedom engulfing us. And in between it all, we still had opportunities to share quality time with mom and the rest of the family. Rob blended easily with my relatives and seemed to be quite at ease with them all. He loved our food and showed his affection for me by often hugging and kissing me in front of everyone. He was also discreet enough to leave mom and I alone when it seemed mom was taking a break from her endless chores. "You need space to talk girl talk" he told me one afternoon when we were at home after lunch. He kissed me, leaving behind the sweet taste of Aunt Mary's rum cake we'd had for desert.

"You two kiss so much" observed mom. "No wonder Rob has that fever blister on his lip"

Rob flinched and instinctively put a finger to his mouth, but then laughed and picked up his Piton beer. "I will leave you ladies to it." Blowing me a kiss, he wandered out of the house into the sunshine. I had noticed the cluster of blisters on his lip had erupted but didn't think anything of it. He had been rubbing ointment on it in the morning and evening. It would soon heal.

Mom pressed me on my relationship with Rob and I told her I was happy.

CHAPTER 6

"More than just happy," I explained, "deeply contented. All I have ever wanted is a good home to bring up two children, a boy and a girl. I want to be able to give them the security you gave me, and some of what you couldn't. I think I can do that with Rob."

After dinner that evening, Rob touched my shoulder. "Let's go for a walk." He said.

I followed him out of the house into balmy warmth of the evening and we walked arm in arm down a few blocks to where a grassy patch ended in a cliff overlooking the bay. We held hands and sat down on the grass to gaze at the lights along the shore below.

"Your family's great" he confided. "They are all so down to earth and natural"

I looked at him with a broad smile; I was flattered that he had adapted to easily. Then he turned to me looking serious

"I love it here Sal" he said dreamily. "This is perfect, I love St Lucia." He took both my hands in his and faced me. "I could live here forever. I could use my engineering skills and get a job planning and maintaining roads. Some of the roads look as though they need work. I could do that."

I smiled. "It's a brilliant idea" I said, "but Rob; there are no jobs in St. Lucia. There's an unemployment problem. Any jobs on offer get taken up by the locals. The budget to fix the roads is slow in coming but it gets done over time. Nobody's in a hurry here."

"Imagine" he persisted, "You, me, Samantha and Christopher, all here on the island like one big happy family, with the rest of your family like a big team."

"That might work if you have a whole bundle of money to invest and start a business that creates employment." I chuckled as I said it. "As an outsider with nothing apart from an obscure technical skill and good intentions to offer, you won't even get a look in."

Rob was quiet for a long time as we sat and stared out at the lights around the bay. Then quite suddenly, he said "Why don't you want me to come and live here with you?" He sounded irritated, almost hostile and I was taken completely off guard. I asked him what he meant.

"This is your home, they can't stop you from coming back." His tone was bordering on confrontational. "If I was to come with you as your partner, they can't turn us away."

I was so surprised by the sudden change in his manner and his persistence, it made me feel uneasy. It was so unlike Rob to display such belligerence.

"Rob," I tried to keep my voice even, "if we came to live here, we would end up being dependant on people who can barely afford to support themselves. You would not be able to find work, and as far as I know, you're certainly not in a position to invest big money into the infrastructure to create employment. It's a wonderful idea, but it's not going to happen."

As suddenly as he had become demanding, his tone softened again to being the gentle soul I loved. He put his arm around me and I relaxed, once again absorbed by his presence and touch. Then he turned and kissed me, deep and passionately.

"We'd better be getting back' he said with a chuckle, breaking away from the kiss. "They'll think we're making love at the top of the cliff."

"It could have happened," I laughed and we walked back to Sofia's house hand in hand.

The vacation drew to an end and I felt an emotional vacuum forming within me at the thought of leaving. I could hardly wait to see Samantha but I was simultaneously saddened by the knowledge it would be at least another year before I'd be back on St. Lucia and among the people I loved so. Saying good bye to mom was especially hard and I could not hold back the tears as we embraced in farewell. Rob also looked somber as he hugged mom and said good bye.

"You look after my little girl" she instructed him with a finger raised in mock rebuke. "She's very special and deserves to be cared for accordingly."

"You can count on it mom" He squeezed her just a little tighter and said "You have taught me so much by just being who you are, and I have loved being here with you more than anything I can remember. Thank you, thank you."

We all had tears in our eyes as Rob and I got into the car and drove back down the Micoud Highway to the airport. Rob reached across and squeezed my hand. "Thank you for bringing me here Sal. It has been the best thing I have ever done."

My heart felt as though it might burst from the pressure of love and contentment contained within its chambers.

There was absolutely nothing to forewarn me of impending events that would change my life in ways I would never have believed possible.

Chapter 7

ROB AND I got back home to New Jersey and I prepared documents and confirmed arrangements for my upcoming surgery. Samantha arrived home the same day and couldn't stop telling us about her camp. She talked non-stop for the whole day of her return. I listened with enthusiasm to her account of adventures and the new friends she'd made at the ten day summer camp, and then told her all about our time at St. Lucia.

We had arrived back in New Jersey on Wednesday 2nd September. My surgery was due on Tuesday 8th, so we decided to take a long weekend and fly to Canada for a visit with my cousin Alana and her husband Sherwin. They were relatives I had told Rob so much about and I really wanted him to meet them.

We toured the city of Toronto and enjoyed good food in their outdoor festivals on the streets. Sherwin is a natural comedian who has an unusual talent to see life in all its forms from a perspective of amusement. He turns every situation into something to be laughed at and it is impossible not to have a great time around him. He is just so entertaining and light hearted, laughter follows wherever he goes.

Toronto is a beautiful city and I love the food, the people

and the environment. It's an indescribably charming place and Samantha informed me that she would be spending her holidays there in future. She made no suggestion as to where the money would come from or who she would stay with, but I didn't upset her dream. Rob enjoyed himself comparing the Toronto beers with the St. Lucia Piton beer. He thought they were both pretty impressive. It turned out a grand weekend. Everything about it was fun and laughter. It was like having two vacations back to back, even though the second was only a 3 day weekend.

We said goodbye to Alana and Sherwin at the airport on the Sunday night and flew back to New Jersey. I felt so totally in tune with Rob and we held hands on the plane feeling as though we had become an extension of each other.

Finally getting home was a good feeling. My surgery would be over within a few days and after recovery, I would have no more trouble with my foot. Life would then return to normal and Rob and I would blend together for a lifetime of happily ever after. It just felt that way.

My time slot was booked for 8.30am, on the 8th of September at Overlook Hospital, New Jersey and I had taken it for granted Rob would drop me off and be there to bring me back home, but while I was unpacking he came in to the bedroom and said he had a problem.

"Tuesday is Christopher's first day of school," he said. "It's important that I'm there for him. His mother will take him to school, but I need to be there to give him a dad's support. I'll have to go there first and come back to take you to the hospital later."

This was the first time he had mentioned anything about Christopher starting school on that day and I couldn't believe he was dropping this piece of information on me now.

"Rob" I said, "why are you telling me this now. We've both know for weeks that my surgery is set for Tuesday. Why didn't you say something about Christopher's school before?'

He didn't look at me, but I could see that quarrelsome attitude emerging, just like the one he had displayed on the cliff above the bay. We'd had such a wonderful time together, I didn't want to spoil anything now but I was suddenly more annoyed than I had been in a long time. Or was it incredulity? Why would he do something like this so deliberately?

"I can't be late Rob," I was trying to remain calm but could feel my face was flushed with displeasure. "You'll have to drop me off first. You can drop me at seven thirty and I'll wait. You can then go to Christopher's school. If I get to the hospital late I could lose my time slot and I can't let that happen. You've known about this since it was first arranged Rob, why is it now that you've decided to tell me about Christopher?"

"I had forgotten until a few minutes ago" he responded, but I could sense he was being evasive. I simply could not fathom what had brought about the sudden change in him. What followed left me speechless.

"You've got your own car," he said staring at me, "why don't you drive yourself and we'll make a plan to fetch your car when you can drive again."

I couldn't believe what I was hearing. What had happened in the last half hour that had altered Rob's attitude like this? Had I missed something or done something to upset him? I couldn't think of what it may have been and chose not to ask. Instead I expressed myself in a way that matched my bewilderment, ignoring the suggestion.

"After you drop me off at seven thirty you'll be able to meet Christopher at his school on time. You can come back to be with me after you've seen him safely into class. You can do that for me can't you?.. Or would that be too much to ask?" I allowed exasperation into my voice.

Rob looked at me almost quizzically, then smiled. "I'm sorry Sal. I'm just a little off balance having just remembered about Christopher's school. Being his first day in the first grade, I think it's important that I'm there." He paused, and then went on. "Of course I'll drop you and come back later. I'm sorry I upset you."

I discovered then I couldn't stay mad at him for long. But this emerging characteristic of sudden mood swings and irrational aggression was a side of him I had only recently been exposed to and it left me feeling uncomfortable. I had witnessed it three times by then and it made me ponder the possibility he harbored a deep seated nature of radical self commitment and split personality syndrome.

That night we watched the movie *'Temptation'* cuddled up on the couch together. All the hostility had evaporated and I felt comfortable in his arms again.

While we were preparing for bed later, Rob was leaning over the basin naked brushing his teeth and I noticed two erupting blisters in the crack of his buttocks. I wondered for the first time why he was prone to what appeared to be fever blisters. I never mentioned it and wasn't really concerned about it.

I was a little nervous about my surgery but couldn't wait for it to be over so I could get back to work. Rob would be there for me as I would for him; It never occurred to me I was living in a vacuum of my own thoughts and dreams. I had allowed myself to fall into an open chamber of euphoria and idealistic expectations. I was about to discover how destructive and careless that was. It had never entered my thoughts at that point, and I would not have believed it anyway if I'd been told I'd fallen in love with a psychopath. But there was worse to come.

I was just an innocent black girl from St. Lucia. In my world, everything would be fine after I checked in at the hospital and had the surgery. Life would return to normal and continue the way it was. Contentment would prevail…… Ignorance is bliss!!

Chapter 8

"MY NAME IS Miss Sally," I said to the receptionist at Overlook Hospital in Summit New Jersey. "I am scheduled for surgery this morning."

She ran a finger down the list on her desk and located my name. "You're nice and early" she said, looking up with a smile. She gave me a sheaf of forms to complete, and directed me to a long shelf like table fixed to the wall on the opposite side of the room. I walked across, sat down on a stool and filled in my details; my insurance company, my employer, my social security number, my doctor's name and address, allergies, any current medication, declaration on heart disease, diabetes, HIV,… and on and on… there were four pages of questions. Under the question: 'Person to be contacted' I filled in Rob's details. Once completed, I took the forms back to the receptionist

"If you wait over there" she pointed to a row of plastic chairs, "someone will be with you shortly." I thanked her and took a seat.

Sitting there on the plastic seats, I felt very alone. Rob had been unusually quiet on the drive to the hospital. He had dropped me off without getting out of the car, and then hurried off to Christopher's school. After watching the movie the night before, we had gone to bed and made love, but I sensed something wasn't right. There was the feeling we were both pre-occupied and I failed to reach an orgasm although Rob didn't have any difficulty. He hadn't demonstrated the tenderness I had become accustomed to with him and once he had satisfied himself made a half hearted token gesture at after play then rolled over and was soon asleep. I hardly slept, worrying about the surgery, but more worried now about what happening in our relationship. I couldn't think of any reason for Rob's sudden coolness after we had shared such unparalleled contentment. Although he had softened and we had cuddled comfortably together and then made love, there was something that didn't feel right. Then this morning, he didn't even bother to wait and make sure I was in the right place before racing off to his son's school which was only a few miles down the road. He would have plenty of time to make sure I was okay and still get to the school with time to spare. His sudden mood swings really concerned me, but I resolved to stay positive. It would pass.

To take my mind off things, I flicked through my Oprah magazine but I was so distracted I put it down, there was no way I could concentrate on reading.

"Miss Sally?" A pleasant matronly woman wearing spectacle with a cord around her neck in a sister's uniform had appeared beside the receptionist and was attaching my forms to a clipboard with a smile.

"That's me" I raised my hand and walked over. Her name badge read 'Robyn Knight.' "Are you OK?" She fixed me with good natured smile and I noticed she wore a small gold cross. Her presence seemed to pour out reassurance and immediately I felt more relaxed.

"Just a little nervous," I replied. "I haven't had surgery

before and I don't know what to expect."

"You'll be fine. These doctors are very good at what they do. I see you've filled in all your papers, so let's go"

"Sure thing." I followed her down a long passage to a ward, where other patients already occupied three of the four beds. I nodded and smiled at them, but I wasn't in the mood for conversation with anybody. Robyn stayed with me.

"Will you call Rob, my boyfriend, when I'm ready?" I asked nervously

"Of course we will"

There was a hospital gown on my bed and I was directed to a cubicle in the corner to change. Pre-op fasting as dictated by the doctor meant I hadn't had anything to eat or drink since 8p.m. the previous evening so my mouth felt like sandpaper and my stomach had gotten over being polite. I sat in the bed and Robyn inserted an IV to keep me hydrated.

She got to making small talk, and I knew she was doing it to keep me calm. She was very professional.

"Have you seen the movie called War Room?" she asked.

I hadn't and shook my head.

"You should go see it" She took my wrist and counted my pulse. "It's very inspirational and well worth the price of a ticket." She took my blood pressure and temperature and nodded, which I assumed meant she was satisfied with the results. "The anesthetist will be here soon" she said. "He'll walk you through the procedure."

She spent a few moments longer putting me at ease and chatting about the movie and I told her I'd go see it as soon as I was mobile again.

"You won't regret it" she said "The power of God is so strong in that movie."

I didn't think about it at the time, but later realised God was trying to talk to me through a nurse and a movie. Robyn had the sort of smile that lights up a face and conveys a message of love. That God given smile gave me the courage I needed to calm down. It was like a magic wand and suddenly I was totally relaxed.

Just after 8.30a.m. Dr. Patel came in to see me. She looked at my charts, nodded with satisfaction then ran me through the procedure once again. She smiled reassuringly the left, saying she'd see me after the op..

Robyn wheeled me to the operating theater and introduced me to the anesthetist, Dr. Hansen. He sat on the end of my trolley and explained his role in the proceedings. He had eyes and a voice that matched each other in kindness. He told me how smooth everything would go and I'd be just fine. I smiled and was pleased everyone involved in the surgery was so reassuring and confident.

"Right, let's get this show on the road" said Hansen. "When I tell you to, I want you to count backwards from twenty," he said.

There was the little scratch on my arm.

"Count. You'll be fine."

I don't know how far I got with the counting, probably not far at all, but the next I knew, I was looking up into the delightful smiling face of Robyn Knight.

"It's OK," Robyn said. "You're back with us. The surgery went well and you'll be back to chasing the children in no time."

"Has Rob called?" I really wanted him to be there.

She shook her head. "Perhaps he got held up at the

school. I'm sure he'll be along shortly"

I was being wheeled back to the ward and my leg was propped up on pillows.

"Keep it elevated as much as you can for the first few days." Robyn thumped her chest lightly. "Higher than your heart. It helps prevents clots and DVT." I wasn't ready for this and dozed off again.

I was awakened by a different nurse much later and realised I had slept most of the day.

"Time to go." Her manner was brusque, an extreme contrast to the kindness Robyn had demonstrated. She was thin with a harsh narrow face and short cropped hair. "Can I call someone for you?"

"Is Rob not here?" It was inconceivable he was not there waiting for me.

"There is nobody here. I'd hardly be asking who I can call if there was someone here waiting for you, now would I?" This woman was unsuited to her profession. I gave her Rob's details, which I knew she already had on the forms I'd completed.

While she was gone I laid back and rested against the pillows, my mind in turmoil. What was happening? Why was Rob not here? What had swung his attitude in a complete one eighty degrees over the past forty eight hours? The questions kept coming and I became more and more anxious and disheartened.

"He'll be here shortly, let's get you dressed." The nurse had returned and was lifting me from the bed with little compassion. Robyn had gone off duty at 3p.m. and had been relieved by this dreadful woman. "Nurse Sandy" according to her name tag.

I was taken in a wheel chair to the reception area where

I had waited earlier in the day. While I waited, I scrolled through my phone. There wasn't a single missed call and no messages. Rob hadn't even tried to reach me. I couldn't believe this was happening.

When Rob arrived, he called my cell. "I'm here." Was all he said.

I was wheeled to the entrance by an orderly and helped into the back of Rob's car where I could rest my foot along the length of the seat. My mood was somber and I felt awkward. My immediate instinct was to challenge Rob, to ask him where he had been, what was happening and why he was being so cantankerous, but I really didn't have the energy to deal with the situation right then. We needed to talk but I would choose the right time and place.

The first night went well. I suspect some of the anesthetic was still in my system, and with the Percocet I coped pretty well. Rob's strange mood seemed to have softened and he was attentive, doing dinner and making sure I was comfortable. I was cautiously optimistic he would get over whatever was bothering him, or that we would at least talk about it and deal with it if it became a problem. Second night was ok, the Percocet kept the pain at bay. Rob remained attentive, bringing me food and caring for me in the way I thought would have been normal between lovers. Samantha also put her bit in and helped around the house. She was picked up by the school bus every morning and dropped off again in the afternoon, so I didn't have to worry about here getting to and from school.

By the third day the effects of the anesthesia had fully

worn off and my pain levels were off the charts. I cried. When I called the doctor, she told me to double the Percocet but I didn't have many left. She said she'd give me a prescription for more, but I'd have to come to the office to get it. "Percocet is a schedule 6 drug" she said "it can't be called into the pharmacy. It can only be given out against a hand prescription." I was sure Rob wouldn't mind.

"Can you go get it for me please?" I asked Rob. I was in tears and not coping. I'd never known such agony. I was unprepared for his response. It just didn't make sense after all we had shared.

"I don't see why I have to go all that way." He said. "Why can't you use my pharmacy?.. My pharmacy is walking distance from the house. Get a prescription for something I can collect without having to drive halfway across the county"

After much pleading, he finally agreed to go. He was really annoyed and pointed out he wasn't my delivery service. He slammed the door on the way out still cursing.

By now I was in tears. The pain I was in, both physically and emotionally, was becoming too much of a burden and I cried in quivering sobs. I was not used to being shouted at. Nobody had ever spoken to me with such malice before. This was the man I loved, yet he was mentally abusing me when I was at my most vulnerable. Nausea from the pain prevented me from wanting to eat. Constipation from the medicine was making me uncomfortable and anxiety from what was happening around me was putting me on edge.

Rob returned with the Percocet half an hour later and without a word went into the kitchen and cooked dinner.

He went the extra mile and made sure I was comfortable and became quite attentive again. The meal smelled delicious with mouth watering aromas coming from the kitchen. I mentally made excuses for Rob's erratic behaviour. Maybe earlier was because we were both tired and stressed. I'd had a bad night and it had probably kept Rob awake as well.

I sat at my usual seat in the dining room and propped my crutches up against the wall. It was innocent and harmless, but Rob snatched them up. "You'll scratch the wallpaper." He said with obvious irritation. "It costs a lot of money and I don't want to have to replace it because of your carelessness." He placed them well out of my reach. "And be careful when you're walking on those crutches, they'll damage my floor."

He sat down at his end of the table. *HIS* floor?.. This was *OUR* home. What was the matter with him? As I looked at him in disbelief, I noticed another fever blister forming at the corner of his mouth.

I didn't know what to do, but my determination to make this relationship work, to understand what had happened to him needed patience. I stared at my plate. The way Samantha looked at me hurt almost as much as his words.

"What's wrong Rob?" I asked looking across at him. "What has happened since we got back from Toronto?... I love you and I hate what is happening here. Talk to me Rob, please!"

He looked across the table at me as if he didn't recognize me. He stared for a moment, and then said. "I just don't want to end up paying for the damage you're doing around here with those sticks"

I was too tired, in too much pain and too humiliated

to respond to him. He cared more about himself and his stupid wall paper than he did about me. I felt unwanted, unimportant. This was the man who had pleaded with me to give up *MY* home to be with him. Now I was being made to feel like an unwelcome guest in *HIS* home. That's not what I had signed up for, but I had come too far to turn back now. We had to work it out. This wasn't the Rob who had come to St Lucia with me and met my mom. He didn't even look the same when he glanced at me. I cried on the inside not wanting Samantha to see my tears. I didn't want to damage her any more than the experiences in her young life already had, but I could see she understood what was going on. Her mom was helpless and hurting and there was nothing she could do about it but watch.

My heart was aching; Had I made a mistake moving in with Rob? Was *this* Rob really the man I would like to spend my life with? What had gone wrong? Why had Rob turned so malicious since our return? How would he react if we were ever faced with a real crisis? Questions tumbled around in my thoughts and the answers were simply not there.

As I got into bed that night I felt like I was in the grip of an anxiety attack. I just couldn't sleep. All I could see was a shadow coming over me and at that stage I was helpless to do anything about it. I knew things could not go on the way they were. It was becoming unbearable.

But the atmosphere being created by Rob got no better. He picked on anything I did to create unpleasantness and I could not get through to him. What made it worse was that I could not fathom what had brought about the change in him. It was less than a week since we'd returned from Canada and it was as if *my* Rob had been abducted and substituted by a look alike with a psychopathic personality disorder. I felt like I needed to get away, but when facing cold reality, I had to concede I had nowhere to go. My car was parked outside, but I couldn't drive. What little money I had would not go far and it was a long way till month end when my wages would be paid. Samantha had just gone back to school after the summer break or I may have considered going to my cousin Anthony or friend Sara in New York. That was out of the question. I felt trapped.... I *was* trapped.

Chapter 9

SOMETHING THAT HAD never so much as occurred to me started giving me cause for concern a few days later. I should have been more attentive to the incident and more assertive in following through on it at the time.

We were in Rob's car on the way to Dr. Patel's rooms for my schedule check up. The pain was under control and I was coping better, but still unable to drive. Rob had reluctantly agreed to take me to my appointment and I was still trying to figure out what had happened to him. He was complaining bitterly about the cost of gas and the drag on his time. He wasn't due back at work after the leave he had taken, until the following Monday. He had originally said he was taking the extra time to be with me after the surgery. Well, as it turned out that was a bad joke. He was grumbling about the inconvenience and I should change my pharmacy if he has to pick up medicine for me, when his mobile phone rang.

The caller was Christopher and Rob quickly picked up. His tone was that of the Rob I had known a week previously. No animosity in his voice. No anger. "Hey Christopher, how are you buddy, what's up?" He listened for a moment, then all the anger came rushing back. I couldn't hear what Christopher was saying, but Rob suddenly hit the brakes and brought the car to a screeching halt. "I'll be there in 5 minutes" he said and ended the call

"That was Christopher. He's still at daycare and his mother's late. That bitch cannot be relied on, I'll have to go and fetch him." He spun the car around and raced away in the opposite direction. My appointment now of secondary importance to him.

"What time should she have been there?" I asked, concerned at the way he had reacted.

"Five thirty. She's so damned unreliable; she shouldn't have custody of my boy"

I checked my watch and saw it was 5.36. She was only six minutes late.

"I need to call Loretta to find out where the hell she is." He called Christopher's mother.

"Where are you?" he demanded. I couldn't hear what she said, but he responded "I'm closer. I'll take him out for dinner and take him home with me. If you can't be on time you shouldn't have custody." Then I did hear her. She shouted down the phone, clearly angry. "I am almost there Rob, just back off".

He cut the call, and accelerated towards the school. He was muttering, almost to himself. "Leaving him at daycare like that. It's abuse. She could have called me to get him, I'll gladly do it but no, she never wants my help. I wish there was something I could do to take my son away from her. She isn't a fit mom. She is always late for everything. I wish I didn't have to deal with her. It's pissing me off"

"She's only six minutes late Rob." I said. "She probably got caught in traffic. It's happened to me before. Why are you making such a big deal about it?.

Rob glared at me. "Are you taking her side?"

"No I am not, it has nothing to do with me, but sometimes things happen that make us a few minutes late. You're making a big deal out of nothing. You're also driving like a road hog."

He didn't respond and we continued the journey in silence. When we reached the school Loretta was right behind us and they both got out of their cars at the same time. I had never seen Loretta before and was surprised at how well groomed and sophisticated she appeared. Christopher was waiting at the gate and she walked across to him, almost bumping into Rob as he tried to get to the child first. That is when I should have been paying attention and been more assertive in following through.

"Are you back on the drugs Rob?" I heard Loretta say. Followed angrily by "Look at me Rob, let me see your eyes." A short pause followed before she said. "You're a fucking idiot Rob, you know damn well what the judge said. I was genuinely pleased for you when I thought you were clean, now you've gone and screwed yourself again. Idiot!!" She took Christopher by the hand and led him to her car, strapped him in then turned and shouted angrily in our direction. "Don't you dare come near my child again until you've sorted yourself out Rob. I will have no hesitation in having you locked up so don't even think about it you hear!" With that she drove away, leaving Rob watching after them, speechless. I was stunned both at the content of the exchange as well as how easily she had cowed him. He stood there watching after Loretta's car like a malevolent child punitively left behind by an ardently admired older sister.

"Is there something I need to know that you haven't told me about?" I asked as Rob got back into the car. He glared at me and what I saw in his eyes made me think I actually had reason to be frightened.

Our journey home was painful on every level: physical, mental, emotional and spiritual.

I closed my eyes and convinced myself it would be alright. We could get through this together. He had a problem he hadn't told me about, but we could work it out. I clung to the loving, kind man who had come with me to St Lucia and Toronto, the man who had met my mom and told her he would look after me. We could get him back. He just needed help.

But he gave me no reason to feel confident in my convictions when we got home. As soon as I sat down he removed my crutches and put them out of reach. It occurred to me he derived some kind of perverse pleasure from my dependence. I couldn't let this go on. It was just on two weeks since we'd returned from our superb trip, a trip through which I had discovered the true meaning of love and contentment. I kept asking myself what had happened, what had gone wrong? Rob wasn't shedding any light on his personality pendulum and after the altercation with Loretta, I was feeling perilously vulnerable.

Chapter 10

WHEN MY FRIEND Sofia, who we'd stayed with in St Lucia called a few days later, a little of the Caribbean sunshine returned to my soul. My foot was much better and the pain had subsided to the point I could put weight on it for short periods. I was trying to get around without the crutches as much as possible. Sofia said she had unexpectedly been invited to spend time in New York and wanted to come and stay with us for a weekend. I was so excited and enthusiastically told her we'd be delighted. I also saw it as an opportunity to calm Rob down.

But when I told him Sofia was in New York and was going to come spend the weekend, he became angry.

"How could you do that without clearing it with me first? How dare you tell her yes it's okay to come over without my permission?" He took a step towards me, the gesture carrying with it a tacit threat. It was the first time his body language had put me on edge. "How would you like it if I invited Frank without asking you? How would you feel?" he snarled.

I stared at him in confusion; Frank was one of Rob's close friends who we saw frequently. Why would I feel anything but happiness for him?

"He's your friend Rob." I said. "I wouldn't mind. Why

should I, especially given the fact I know him and have visited his house." Then I swallowed my fear of this angry man and stood up to him. "Rob, we spent nine days in Sofia's house in St Lucia less than three weeks ago. She fed us; she showed us genuine hospitality and invited us back whenever we wanted to go there. She treated you with kindness and made you feel entirely at home. What is the matter with you? I had no idea you would object. Why are you being like this?" He was making it clear he didn't want anyone coming to see me in his house. "What has happened to you, Rob?" I pleaded. "Where has the Rob I fell in love with gone?.. Where is he?. What has happened to him?" I burst into tears and hobbled out of the room.

A few minutes later he came to me and for the first time since our return from Canada, I saw the Rob I wanted to share my life with.

"I am sorry I've behaved so badly," he said, taking me in his arms. "I have a lot going on in my head and it is making me say and think crazy things." He took me in his arms and kissed me. I was so overwhelmed I kissed him back, craving the love we had known and wanting him to know I was still his. It came as a surprise to me just how much I wanted this man who had shown me such cruelty and disrespect, and I kissed him with all the passion in my heart. When we broke away, he held me close to him and I wanted to weep.. "Please Rob," I pleaded, "let's talk about the crazy things going on in your head. Let's work it out together. We were so happy. Let's bring that happiness back. I love you." He smiled at me soothingly, gave me a squeeze and kissed me on the forehead before turning away without another word. It fell short of the reassurance I was hoping for.

Sofia arrived on Friday evening to spend the weekend

and brought my spirits almost back to normal. She cooked, she cleaned, she straightened up, and she did the laundry. She helped out as much as she could while we chatted and chuckled endlessly. Rob went back to work on that Saturday, and I told her nothing of his transformed character since our return. We needed to work that out between us. Sofia took on the roll of nurse, taking care of me as if I were an invalid. She made sure I took my medicine and rested as per doctor's orders, and we laughed together over past events and people we'd known.

Sofia and I went back a long way and our friendship was cast in stone. It was hard for me not to share with her my anxiety over Rob's change in character, but I kept it to myself. While we chatted, we were looking at an article in a magazine where a thousand dollars was up for grabs as a prize in a promotion on 106.7fm, one of our local radio stations. Tongue in cheek we entered online and put all our names in, including Rob's. We had a good giggle, but agreed it was unlikely we would win it and promptly forgot about it.

Sofia's stay was far too short. She took such care of me while she was there and was like a breath of fresh air after the stifling atmosphere between Rob and I. We always had a lot to talk about and when we were together our laughter was rich and from the soul. Rob had volunteered to work through Sunday and hardly made an appearance the whole weekend. Sofia had to get back to New York and she took a cab to the train station just after 5.00p.m. Her departure left a void in my soul coupled with apprehension. I had started to dread Rob's presence. He was so unpredictable and I felt like I needed someone else close to defuse the volatile atmosphere.

But saying goodbye to Sofia wasn't the only emotionally painful event at the end of that weekend. She had barely driven away in the cab when my mobile rang and the caller ID came up as Kate Howard. The first thought I had was how nice it was of her to call.

"Hi Kate" I said putting a smile into my voice, "this is a nice surprise"

"Hi Sally" She sounded all business, not like this was a social call. "How are you getting along after the surgery?"

"Still pretty painful, but each day is better. I'm walking without my crutches on and off. I'll be ready to come back to work on schedule"

There was an audible sigh from here end, followed by an ominous silence. Then she said, "Well that's partly the reason for my call Sally, and there is no easy way to say this so I'll just tell it like it is. We don't need your services any more. There have been some unexpected changes since you've been away and it's forced us to cut back on our expenses. It tears me apart to be giving you this news, but we simply cannot afford to keep two nannies for the children. I am so sorry. We'll pay you what is owed to you in wages for the month, but when you get better you should find another job. I am so sorry."

I sat with the phone pressed against my ear, not wanting to believe what I was hearing. I'd loved that job and had come to love the children almost as if they were my own. That alone was enough to bring tears to my eyes, but the blow of being fired was like someone had just sucked all the air out of me, leaving me bereft of senses or sensations. I was suddenly numb. Kate was still talking, but I wasn't hearing her. All I could think of was what else could be thrown at me to push me down, to drain my spirits of contentment. Why were so many cruel twists of fate forcing their way into my life? What had I done to deserve being emotionally tortured first by Rob, now with the loss of my job? I had done everything expected of me. I had loved unconditionally. I had gone the extra mile in being the best person I could be. I had never so much as wished harm on another living soul, now I was being tormented and crushed by unexpected and undeserved events and being forced into a state of despair.

"Are you there?" I heard Kate say.

"Yes Kate, I'm here. I can't say I'm in one piece, but I'm here. I need to adjust to what you've just told me, but I'll be okay. Thank you for calling"

I heard her say "I'm so sorry" as I cut the call. This was not going to be easy. I'd loved my job and needed the income that came with it. It was all I had to support Samantha in a way my real parents had never supported me. Furthermore, I'd been having doubts about my future with Rob. Our relationship was so unpredictable it was as though I was walking on eggshells most of the time, and I was worried about Samantha being subjected to the constant undercurrent of hostility in the house. My job had been my backup security. Now it was gone.

With Sofia on her way back to New York, Rob still at work and Samantha at Peter's for the weekend, I was entirely alone, gripped by a sense of isolation and despair. The emotions welled up within me and I could not hold back the tears. All the tension of the past three weeks, all the anxiety, the rift between Rob and me, all the pain both physical and emotional all burst to the surface and I wept. Heart wrenching shoulder shuddering sobs engulfed me and hollowed me out. How could this be happening?.... What was happening ??. How could providence have intervened and brought me down so swiftly? Only three weeks previously I had been as happy and carefree as anyone could wish to be. Now it was as if some rogue celestial puppeteer with a cruel vendetta had discovered my happiness and was spitefully pulling the strings of destiny, stripping away the euphoria of my blissful existence. From Rob's puzzling transformation, to the surgery which I had never expected to be as painful or as complicated, and now this..... I was unlikely to find another job any time soon in my present condition, and I suddenly became acutely aware of the downside to being paid directly without agency backup. Kate and Barry had paid me "off the books" and although I'd taken care of my own tax returns, I had no agency protection or employment contract against unfair dismissal. I suspected an ulterior motive as Kate's claim of financial problems and being unable to afford me didn't ring true. They frequently spent more on a single dinner party than they paid me in a month, and Barry's company wasn't losing money. I felt cheated at all levels. I suddenly couldn't wait for Rob to get home. I needed to talk and I hoped I could confide in him and we'd work out a solution together. I still had faith in being able get to the bottom of the rift that had developed between us.... I was still naïve and clinging to the dream Rob had represented.

I was able to get around the house without my crutches most of the time. The pain was subsiding, and I had cut down on the dosage of Percocet. Putting weight on my foot was tender, but no longer torture. It had been almost three weeks since the surgery and I had believed I would be back at work by the following week. Well, that idea had

CHAPTER 10

gone under the executioner's axe and I felt as though part of my insides had been ripped out along with the blow.

When Rob walked in from work, I hadn't moved from the couch where I had been sitting when I cut the call from Kate. He came to me and kissed me on my forehead, then looked at me more closely.. "What's happened?" he put his hands on either side of my face. "You've been crying."

Inside I was still crying. Crying like a baby and Rob's words brought on a fresh burst of emotion. For several minutes I couldn't speak and Rob sat down beside me. He didn't embrace me, made no physical attempt to comfort me, he didn't even ask. He just sat there beside me and let me cry. Eventually I pulled myself together enough to blurt out "They fired me, Rob."

"Oh no" he responded, finally putting his arm around me. He held me for no longer than a minute while I sobbed quietly into his chest, then he stood up and moved towards the bedroom to get out of his work clothes. "What will you do?" he was walking away as he talked. "Will you get another job soon?" There was no hint of distress in his tone. It was if I'd told him the neighbors had popped in to say hello and he'd just missed them. At that moment I felt my heart turn to stone... Who was this man?

I pulled myself together as best I could "Of course, I will." Tears were running down my cheeks. "I've never been without a job. I've always worked…. Always been able to look after myself" I added.

"OK." He walked into the bathroom to shower. All I'd wanted was to feel like he cared; just a gesture of comfort

67

and support, but that was too much for him.... Who was this man, where had *my* Rob gone? How could I go on living like this??

I got up off the couch and walked to the bathroom. I had to have it out with Rob, I had to find out what had gotten into him since we'd returned from Toronto, I needed to clear the air. I pushed the door open and froze.

On the vanity stand was a small hand mirror with a slim line of white powder sprinkled across it. I probably wouldn't have noticed it, had it not been for the fact that Rob was bent over it with a short straw up his nose sucking in the powder off the mirror. For a brief moment I wasn't aware of what I was witnessing and then it came crashing in on me. Loretta had accused Rob of being "back on the drugs." Other than to try getting out of Rob what she meant, I hadn't pursued it and he had been offhandedly vague. Now I knew exactly what she had meant. Rob was in our bathroom snorting cocaine.

I'm not sure exactly what happened immediately in the wake of my unexpected entrance. I have a vague recollection of Rob jerking up straight, trying to put a hand over the mirror, and me lunging forward to knock it off the stand. It was a small room, one stride would have got me to my target but my head suddenly exploded in a flash of white light and my legs folded beneath me. There was a strange sensation of disorientation and then a second crack against my head which I later learned was my head coming into contact with the edge of the bath.

Being knocked unconscious leaves a metallic taste in the mouth and a sensation of bewilderment in the mind. Rob swears blind he never raised a hand to me but there is no other possible explanation why I experienced a blinding light and jelly legs when I was within two feet of him. I never saw the blow coming and have no recollection of Rob's hand being anywhere near me, but it was a confined space and I was focused on the line of coke on the vanity stand. It can only have been him hitting me causing me to fall in the first place.

Regaining my senses, my first impression was of Rob staring down at me. He was pale with a look of anguish. His hair was ruffled as though he had been repeatedly running his hands through it. His eyes were wide and I could feel him shaking through a damp towel he was holding against my head. I was lying on the bathroom floor, my head throbbing, my mouth as dry and gritty as desert sand and I felt nauseous. There was painful swelling at the side of my face. Rob's naked torso was covered in blood and I knew it was not his blood. I had no idea how long I had been out cold, but from that moment I knew I had to get away from this man. As far away as possible. I had never felt so alone or so exposed to danger..

"Are you alright?" were his first words. "You fell and hit your head against the bath."

He was babbling like an underage drinker trying to explain why he was holding an open bottle of booze and stinking of liquor.

"You hit me Rob. You hit me so hard it knock me out, that's why I hit my head on the bath.

"I swear Sal, I didn't touch you. You fell."

I was not convinced but was in no position to argue and I didn't want to antagonize him. I'd walked in on him snorting coke in our bathroom and he had reacted violently. I was still in a daze but my thoughts were clear. Samantha and I were in a fix. The reality was that we were trapped.

Samantha had to go to school; I was now unemployed and we had nowhere else to live. More for Samantha than for myself I had to keep a roof over our heads but we were dependent on a psychopathic coke user.

For the first time in my life I was truly scared.... Who was this man I had fallen in love with? I had been so sure of him, so sure of myself. We had blended so perfectly, like the instruments of a symphony orchestra. So beautifully in tune.... What had gone wrong? What had I missed? What had triggered the schizophrenia? ...What was I going to do? ...

I closed my eyes and the tears once again defeated my best efforts to hold them back. I lay there on the cold bathroom floor and cried inconsolably. My thoughts went back to that night six years previously when Peter had told me of his affair and my world had come crashing in on me. Now it had happened again, but I was so much more vulnerable now.

Rob remained attentive to my condition. He helped me to my feet and guided me to the bedroom. I sensed the incident had unnerved him. He'd clearly got one hell of a fright and his remorse showed in his demeanor. He seemed nervous, as if he were afraid some kind of retribution was about to befall him.

I inspected my wounds in the bedroom mirror. I was going to look a bit like a prize fighter for a few days, but the damage was not serious. The 'gash' on my head turned out to be nothing more than a cut which had poured out a disproportionate amount of blood. The bleeding had stopped although a purple 'egg' had formed around it. The bruised swelling on the other side of my face, (where I suspect Rob's punch had landed), would be gone in a week.

God knows, I had time on my hands and didn't need to go out anywhere. To this day I have never told Samantha or anyone else what really happened. By way of explanation, my crutch had slipped on the wet bathroom floor and not being able to use my hands to steady myself, I had been bashed about a bit on the way down. The story was an acceptable one. My circumstances were not!!

I needed a way out and I cautiously started considering my options.

As of that afternoon, I was unemployed. I had recently spent on air tickets to St. Lucia and Toronto, (my treat for Rob), enough to have seen us through about three months living expenses. The ticket purchases had left me with little more than enough to feed us for a month. My month's wages from Kate & Barry had not yet been paid and once I had that in my account I could extend providing for Samantha and myself for another month. I had my car, but at that stage I was considering it as a possible means of temporary accommodation for the two of us. If I were to sell it, I would be worse off than I had been when I first arrived in America and it would take me years to replace it. The car was an asset I could not afford to be without. Peter's contribution towards child care had not seen an increase in nearly four years and was inadequate anyway, so there was no relief there. I needed to get back with the agency as a means of finding a new job. I was aware that after not having been on their books for almost eighteen months, I would be placed right at the bottom of the list of candidates and that was a concern. There was no quick fix there. I could take Samantha out of school and move back to New York, where my cousin Anthony had an apartment in the Bronx. I had an open invitation to go there if ever I needed a place.

Disrupting Samantha's schooling in an attempt solve my problems seemed like a good way to add to my problems. She had settled in where she was and had made a lot of friends. Piled on top of my list of solution resistant troubles was my current state of mobility. It would be at least another week, perhaps two before I could feel comfortable for any length of time without crutches and applying for a job under those conditions would be a waste of time.

For now, we had a roof over our heads, albeit in an atmosphere of tension and hostility. Samantha's schooling was in hand and her transport to and from was routine. I had bought groceries and stocked the larder before my surgery so we had food to eat, at least for a now. But I had made the decision our current living arrangements were to be temporary. I would move into Samantha's room with her and as soon as I could, we would leave and restart our lives independently. The tension weighing in on me was agonizing, and the disturbing undercurrent of emotional confusion constantly threatened an out pouring of uncontrollable tears. It was as if my stomach had been tied in a knot, ensnaring a stirring of nervousness. I had never been so miserably unhappy. The constant pressure was taking me down.

While we were in St. Lucia, I had believed without question, Rob would stand by my side and support me in any circumstances or situation. As realistic as those expectations had been at the time, they had proven to be a dream too far three weeks later.

Chapter 11

ONCE THE POST op bruising on my foot had cleared I started physiotherapy. It was coming up a month since the operation and a month of being forced to live under a cloud of unremitting hostility and tension. When my living dream had been at its most intense, when Rob and I had been together in St. Lucia, the mere thought of push back or protest from him would not have emerged. Now, I decided I wasn't even going to ask him to help me. I had reached the stage where I could drive myself and use the crutches between the car and the therapist's rooms.

Day by day I could feel the improvement and was soon not using the crutches at all. Three days a week of therapy with the therapist showing me the exercises to do at home, and I felt confident I could start looking for a job.

I was playing it carefully in the house. I had moved my clothes into Samantha's room and slept there on cushions on the floor. When I told Rob I was doing that, he'd all but helped me pack. We coexisted under the same roof but hardly spoke to each other. I prepared the meals and if Rob was home to eat he'd join us in stoic silence. If he wasn't, I'd leave his meal in the warmer. His presence at the dinner table was becoming less and less frequent.

When we needed supplies from the supermarket, I

would pay for them but my money was going to run out and I needed to tell Rob what we needed. He would reluctantly give me fifty or twenty dollars and never fail to throw in a hurtful comment like "Bring me all my change." Or "I want to see the till slip. Don't think you can cheat me by throwing it away."

His comments made me feel cheap and helpless. I'm still not sure how frequently his drug habit messed up his mind, I had distanced myself from him to the extent I didn't care, but he made me feel like a child. My dependence on him had become a source of humiliation and shame. I'd never had to beg for anything and the experience felt like a disgrace. This was not what I wanted for myself or my daughter. I felt cowed, and subservient. Whenever I was alone my despair would consume me and fighting back tears was becoming an increasingly difficult feat. I couldn't work out the sudden change in Rob. It had occurred almost from one minute to the next when we returned from Canada. I had constantly wracked my brains to pinpoint anything that gave him cause, something I had done? Yet the more I thought about it the further away I seemed to be from answering the multitude of questions. And Mom's voice kept coming back to me "People will let you down. God never will." And I cried even more.

One night after Samantha had gone to bed and I was alone in the lounge, Rob came home in high spirits. He appeared as he had done on all those occasions I had looked at him and thought how lucky I was to have him. He was friendly and chatty and wanted to know about my day and if there had been any break through on the job front. Did I need anything?... His whole character had reverted to the kind, evenly spoken person I had been so attracted to the first time we had met. The transformation was astonishing. He asked about Samantha and said he felt guilty for not having taken more interest in her wellbeing.

I was amazed. It was almost as if the Rob I had fallen in love with, the one I had gone to St.Lucia and Toronto with, had slipped away leaving behind a stand in with a personality defect, but the real Rob had now returned, completely ignorant of the abuse and cruelty his substitute had subjected me to... This was eerie.

"Rob" I was looking into his eyes, trying to see beyond the surface. "what has happened to you?... Is this the real you, or is that other creature the person I'm stuck with?"

"Aww c'mon Sal, I've had a few things on my mind that have caused me to be a bit distracted. Work related stuff and issues with Loretta, but there's no need for those things to have an effect on us"

This was too much. "No need for them to have an effected on us?" I echoed raising my voice. "Rob for the past month you have treated me like a piece of baggage you picked up off the street and couldn't wait to put back there. You've abused my trust in you, you've psychologically abused Samantha, you've insulted me, punched me although you won't admit to that. You've made my life here a living hell. How can you come in here and tell me what you've done should not have an effect on us?... Are you mad?"

He patiently sat there and let me pour out my anger and then smiled the slow, irresistible smile that lit up his eyes and had usually been effective in getting me aroused before he even touched me.

"It's okay Sal, I understand you're mad at me, but didn't we almost have it all?" he was quoting a line from a song I adored. "We can take it back Sal. We can rewind and take it all back."

"I don't think we can Rob." I was trying to get my head around what was happening. "Too much damage has been done.. Tell me about the drugs Rob. Tell me why you never mentioned that. Tell me why I had to find out the way I did. Tell me about the problems at work and the problems with Loretta.. Tell me about your *life* Rob. Tell me the things I need to know about a man who I gave my entire heart and soul to without conditions.. Tell me why I should even be having this conversation with you" I felt strength in my argument but weakness in my heart and I sensed the emotions creeping into my voice and into my eyes.

He came over and sat beside me. He put an arm over my shoulder and drew me to him. He smelled the way I remembered him. The aroma associated with love and passion. The overwhelming yet mysteriously odorless fragrance of testosterone. He put his mouth close to my ear. "We don't have to live in the past Sal. We can make a new beginning without all that in the way."

I was so tempted to turn to him and kiss him in a way that left no doubt as to how much I wanted that, but although the lust was there, the trust was gone. If it was ever going to be regained, it would take a whole lot more than two minutes of sweet talk when I was at my most vulnerable. This man had shown me two sides of himself and the heartbreak I was already suffering could only be made worse by allowing myself back into his complicated and unpredictable clutches. Besides that, I suspected the motivation behind his show of compassion and reconciliation was nothing more than a short term need for sex.

"If we're ever going to make a new beginning Rob, you're going to need to go for help. You're a classic bipolar case, you're a drug user and as things are, I see you as potentially dangerous. There will be no new beginning while that baggage stands between us"

"Well fuck you" he blurted. "What the fuck are you and your brat doing in my house if that's the case". I had flipped the switch and the schizophrenia had activated. "I never asked you to come here. You just fucking moved into my life uninvited. I was perfectly okay before you came here. I want you out you hear? I don't have to put up with your shit."

His anger was so intense he'd gone red in the face his eyes were bulging. He had gotten up off the couch and was standing facing me waving his arms in gestures from the bedroom to the front door.

I stood up and glared at him. "You know every aspect of that last statement is a blatant lie Rob. Don't you dare insult my daughter or me ever again you hear?... And yes!!... We will be moving out, just as soon as it suits us. You disrupted our lives by bringing us here, you can just back off while we work out how to put them back together. And don't you dare ever lay a hand on me again. You will live to regret it."

My nerves were like violin strings and my heart was pounding. I was unsure of my limits or if he would react violently if I crossed them. I remembered how he had been cowed by Loretta as soon as she stood up to him and it seemed to work for me as well. He just stood there staring at me, all the bravado and bluster was gone. But I was still in *HIS* house. That needed to change.

I walked into Samantha's bedroom and locked the door behind me. I sat on the edge of her bed trembling, trying not to disturb her. I just needed somewhere to sit.

"Mommy, I'm scared" I was startled by her tiny voice. I had thought she was asleep. The intensity of the fear in her young voice slammed into my heart like a sledge hammer and the tears rolled over my eyelids and down my cheeks. What had I exposed this poor innocent child to?

"Don't be scared Sammy" I tried not to let my voice crack. "We'll find a way."

At that moment I could easily have put my hands around Rob's throat and strangled him without a conscience, but was reminded again of Mom's advice. "Put your trust in God.. People will let you down, God never will."

I lay down beside Samantha and took her in my arms holding her close, willing strength into her. "We'll find a way, I promise!"

I closed my eyes and drew my child closer, silently begging God to help me find a way out of our trapped existence. It had been a long time since I had prayed, but God would have had no difficulty recognizing my earnestness. My prayers came from deep in the soul and were offered up unconditionally with purpose, pleading and desperation. I had never been as sincere in all my life.

As usual, sleep did not come easily. The turmoil in my mind and in my heart would not allow contented rest. I was constantly on edge and mindful of how bad things were for us. We would soon be out of money and foolish pride would not allow me to reach out to friends or relatives. There was no shortage of either, but I had not confided in any of them about the break down in our relationship or the dire straits I was facing. Besides, they had their own lives to live with their own issues. None of them were financially able to take on my problems. I couldn't impose on them to bale me out of my predicament. It just wouldn't be right....It was up to me to find a solution.

I had put my name down at the nurses and nannies agency I had worked for previously but had not heard a word from them. I had gone online and registered with as many other agencies as I could find. I had even followed up on an idea Sofia and I had laughed about when we saw an advertisement in a magazine we were looking at. It was for "sophisticated ladies willing to escort visiting gentlemen to corporate engagements"... It had shocked and horrified me when the reality of that kind of work had been explained to me.... I had no idea where to turn and there was no end to the tears and torment. The nights were long and torturous and knowing the potential long term effects Samantha could suffer as a result of our situation did not make it any easier. It was as if the weight of the whole world was pressing down on me, clawing at my sanity, testing the limits of my endurance.

As the eastern sky showed the first signs of light, I could hear Rob moving about in the house getting ready for work. It had been a protracted, restless night of tossing and turning, and I was unsure if I had slept at all. I dreaded another day of uncertainty, tension and dependence. I had no desire to encounter Rob so remained unmoving and silent. Suddenly there was a loud banging on the door immediately followed by Rob's raised voice. "I can't support three people. I have no obligation to you two. I want you out you hear?.. I want you out of my house."

I chose to keep quiet and gestured to Samantha by putting a finger to my lips. I was not going to get into a verbal scrap that early in the day, particularly not with Samantha looking on. Let him rant on. Let him go to work. I'd be ready for him when he came back. It occurred to me how wonderful it would be if I could fix it so he came home to an empty house, stripped of any trace we had ever been there. When circumstances changed in my favour, that was exactly what I planned to do. But I knew it wasn't going to happen on that particular day.

What did happen on that particular day was as unexpected as it was undeserved and made me wonder whose side God was on. Samantha was at school and I was doing the household chores, something Rob never acknowledged nor ever seemed to notice and I had the radio on 106.7fm. I wasn't really listening, it was just music in the background, but suddenly my ears pricked up as I heard Rob's name being announced.

"And this month's winner of one thousand dollars, we congratulate Mr. Robert......." I could hardly believe my ears, this was the competition Sofia and I had entered and included Rob's name. I hadn't even told Rob we had entered. My first thought was 'what a travesty'. I had entered the competition, I had put Rob's name in, I hadn't told him about it and I needed that thousand dollars a whole lot more than he did. The presenter had gone on;

"Robert, you have twenty minutes to call in and claim your prize or we move on to the next contestant and your prize will be forfeit, so get your fingers to the phone and give us a call."

I was tempted to call in and try my luck at claiming the prize without Rob ever knowing, but it was a passing thought. I'd no sooner let it pass when Rob called me on my mobile. He was upbeat and sounded a lot more

CHAPTER 11

congenial than he had earlier that day when he was banging on my door telling me to get out of his house.

"I just heard on the radio I won a thousand dollars. Did you enter me in that competition?"

"A thousand dollars?... WOW" I said. "That's nice, and yes, I did enter you in the competition. Sofia, who you didn't want here, remember?, she and I did it while she was here over the weekend you hardly made an appearance. What do you have to do to claim it?"

"I need to call in within twenty minutes. Wow Sal, thank you. I need that cash"

With that he cut the call and a few minutes later I heard his voice on the radio. To his credit, he did tell whoever was listening that it was a surprise and that I had entered his name without him knowing. He referred to me as his "girlfriend." I wasn't sure if I was comfortable with that

"Well that good lady of yours sure deserves a slap up dinner and a night on the town Robert. Be sure to spoil her with kindness."

'Yeah, right!!' I thought. 'Those days are gone.'

I was right. When the check arrived by courier a few days later, he flaunted it as though it was his just reward for completing a drawn out and difficult assignment. He offered an unconvincing gesture of thanks to me for entering his name but at no time was there a suggestion we could share the prize. I so needed $500.00 right then, possibly more than I had ever needed it at any time in my entire life before or since. Rob knew it (or maybe he didn't). One thing was for sure; He didn't care. As far as he was concerned, it was his and his alone. I had played no part in it.

December and the holidays were approaching. I wasn't going to be in a position to buy Christmas gifts for anyone. Samantha's birthday was also in early December and I had to explain to her that as I wasn't working I wouldn't be able to buy her a gift. It tipped the delicate balance of my emotions when she hugged me and said "Mommy I love you and I know how hard it is for you to take care of me. I know it's temporary and it will get better".

I held her in my arms and began to cry. In so many ways I was blessed. Despite the horror of my situation, I had this amazing little person in my life who understood what I was going through. I raised my head to the heavens and said a prayer to God. Thanking him for blessing me with this child.

Chapter 12

AS IT TURNED out, Peter had decided to host a party for Samantha's 10th birthday. When he told me about it, he said Rob was welcome to attend and to bring Christopher. I had told Peter about Rob before we went to St. Lucia, but they had never met. Peter had no idea of the rift between us and I hadn't enquired about how things were working out between Rob and Loretta after the altercation outside the school. He hadn't volunteered any information on the subject. Our relationship wasn't exactly conducive to exchanging chitchat about the welfare of his alienated son or the restrictions his ex-wife had placed on his visitation rights. Frankly, I didn't want him anywhere near Samantha's birthday party. If I had it my way, I would have him anywhere near either of us. I still hadn't told anyone of the breakdown in our relationship and chose to play it down by telling Rob about the party in such a way it was not framed as an invitation. We were after all still technically living together, albeit under circumstances of duress and conflict, but nobody else knew that.

When the day arrived, Rob decided he would come with us to the party; in fact he was quite insistent upon coming. I couldn't think why he would want to do that. He had shown no interest in anything we did and we lived as if there was a barrier between us. More accurately, we lived as if we were in separate houses. The only verbal contact we had was his frequent enquiries as to when we would be moving out. "I want you out of my house" was an almost daily reminder of the fact we were not welcome guests. I responded by telling him we wouldn't be there in the first place if I had known in advance of his inability to hold a relationship together. "We'll be gone as soon as possible" was my stock reply and my heart groaned under the weight of the tension. Now he wanted to come with us to the birthday party of a child he made no secret of despising. Just another aspect of his disturbed frame of mind is what I thought. I told him he would probably want to leave early and as it was Samantha's party she would want to stay until the end. If he attended, he would have to go in his own car. That's what he did.

The event was like a princess welcoming party. I was hugely impressed and equally surprised at the job Peter had done and how well organized it was. There was an awesome turn out of kids and their parents. He had hired a jumping castle and a clown who doubled as a magician and had the children spellbound making items disappear and reappear and then performing in awe of himself, bringing out peels of youthful laughter. There was an abundance of sodas and a huge variety of cookies and a birthday cake adorned with ten colourful candles. Peter had insisted he take care of everything and consequently, I hadn't played any part in putting it together. That saddened me, but at the same time I was delighted at the

CHAPTER 12

effort Peter had put in to make Samantha's tenth birthday a memorable occasion. The marvelous sound of kids laughing and enjoying themselves was like a tonic. I was thrilled to see Sammy have so much fun. It would take her mind off our existence under Rob's roof if nothing else and I was grateful for that.

Contrary to the cheerful activities all around him, Rob had isolated himself in a corner and was looking like the picture of gloom. He was so obviously in a mindset of misery it glowed. As I watched him it became clear to me why he had insisted on coming. He had wanted to see where Peter lived and what sort of spread the party would provide. I could practically read his mind. 'Why were we living in his house eating his food if Peter could lay on such a grand party?'

I didn't have to wait long for confirmation. I went across to him and, in honour of the occasion, tried to make light of it. "Cheer up Rob," I smiled. "It might never happen"

Speak of a wasted effort; He looked at me as if I had just stripped him of his identity and all his possessions. "You can stop pretending you have nowhere else to live now" he scowled. "It's clear you've been lying to me. Your daughter can come and live with her father. He can obviously afford it. I can't. You can go to your aunt."

"Don't turn this into an unpleasant occasion in an attempt justify your moral bankruptcy Rob. I'll discuss it with you later." I turned away angrily before he could respond, but noticed Peter had been watching the exchange from across the room. He looked at me quizzically and then turned to talk to someone else. I suspected he'd figured from our body language, all was not hugs and happiness. I was in two minds if I wanted him to know or not.

It was a wonderful party and Samantha's day had been one of love and laughter. It gave me so much pleasure to watch her enjoying herself the way she did. That was the kind of happiness I wanted her to experience every day. Living with Rob made that nigh on impossible. He seemed to be going out of his way to be as unpleasant as possible and to make the lives of those around him as miserable as his own.

Samantha stayed with Peter after the party and I went home alone anticipating an ugly scene I didn't want her to witness. To spoil her day after having been so happy for a change would have been unacceptable. The first thing Rob did as I walked in the door was to remind me we were unwelcome in his house.

"I am not giving you anymore money" like he ever gave us money. "You're not my problem and not my responsibility. I just need you out of my house. We're not married, I don't owe you anything. Get out of my house or I'll call the cops." He had been at the drugs again and had a can of beer in his hand. He didn't look great.

Whether it was the drugs and the booze, or a deep seated prejudice he had concealed was not clear, but what he said next shocked me to the point I couldn't believe I'd heard him correctly.

"I don't want niggers living in my house, you're all bloody thieves and I don't want to be contaminated with any diseases."

We had been lovers in a way that made the earth move for 8 weeks before his transformation. We had lived under the same roof for almost 4 months and at no time had the issue of race ever even been a topic of conversation. His sudden outburst of racist insults caught me so off balance it made my head spin.

"What did you say?" I demanded. I was so angry I spat the question out. "Did you just call me a nigger?"

He just stood there staring at me. His eyes didn't seem to focus and he swayed slightly. "Yeah!" his speech had a rasp and a slur to it. "You're a nigger and I don't want you or your nigger kid living here anymore. I need you to make money to pay your way. You can't do that but your nigger kid has a father who seems okay. I'm done caring for you." He turned and walked to his bedroom. I was speechless and leant against the kitchen counter for support. My instinct was to go after him and smash my fist into his arrogant face. I wanted to do something that would inflict excruciating pain on him but I sat and watched as he went into his room and slammed the door. The tears welled up in me and I sobbed my frustration and anger into my hands. I had to get out of this toxic environment.

As I sat there seething, my spirits so low I felt utterly crushed, the sound of an incoming sms message bleeped. It wasn't my phone, but then I noticed Rob had left his mobile on the counter. I reached across and idly looked at the display. 'Katy'… I wondered who Katy was and out of curiosity opened the message. I really didn't care if I was invading his privacy. When I read the message I was aghast. "Hey there big boy.. I bet you'd love to know what I'm not wearing. (smileyface)… Well you're going to have to get over here to find out.".... There were previous messages on the thread and I scrolled up to read them. There were texts telling her how cute and beautiful she was. This was during the time he'd been doing everything he could to make me feel ugly and unattractive. Nothing had been deleted and the messages were dated back to September.

That was when I had my surgery. He was texting this woman within days of us getting back from our amazing vacation. I scrolled back to the beginning again.

"Hi there, it's Katy. Care to chat?"

"Yeah sure. Why not. Where do you live?"

"Elizabeth New Jersey.. You?"

"We're practically neighbors. Nice coincidence"

The messages went on with increasing familiarity between them, reaching into the suggestive and then into the intimate and erotic. There was a plan brewing for them to meet for a date on the upcoming Saturday at the same restaurant I had met him for the first time.

The truth dawned on me and I went cold. The bastard!!.., I had been nothing more than a conquest for him. He'd gotten tired or bored so he'd started to treat me like something the cat had brought in and moved on to someone else. Before I looked at his phone I was so over Rob, if I'd never seen him again in my life it would have been too soon. But those messages got to me. It was as though I'd been slapped in the face and stripped naked in a public park for anybody passing by to piss on me. The humiliation, the sense of self degradation made me shiver. Dirt seemed to ooze out of my pores and crawl over my skin like a rash and I experienced a depth of loathing entirely foreign to my character.

I'd paid to take him to St. Lucia, I'd introduced him to my family and had given of myself from the depth of my soul. I'd taken him to Toronto without the slightest inkling that by then he was already flirting elsewhere. It all made sense now. I'd been played for a patsy from the beginning and as reality set in, the fury rose in me like an active volcano which then erupted with an involuntary bellow.

CHAPTER 12

"YOU BASTARD!!" I yelled. "I HATE YOU".

I expected him to come out of his room then and I was going to kill him, but the door remained closed.

I held the phone, staring at the screen with tears streaming down my face in uncontrollable torrents of shame and disgust. Then on impulse I pressed the call key. She answered on the second ring. "Hi big boy are you here already?" There was such a seductive smile in her husky voice I could almost smell the pheromones.

"Sorry to disappoint you Katy," I was battling to keep my voice even but losing. "This is not big boy, this is Sally, his live in nigger whore" I let out a sob.

There was a silence on the other end and I let it hang for a moment then went on.

"I'm calling to let you know that I've read through all your text messages and noticed he's failed to point out that he's a psychopathic drug addict who is prone to becoming violent during sex." That wasn't true but it sounded good. "He likes to hurt vulnerable women." That evidently was true and I was a victim. "I just thought you might like to know. Oh and by the way, he gets tired of his women real quick. Ask me, I found out the hard way."

The silence hung like a pending storm and then she sighed loudly.

"Oh my God, I had no idea. He told me he was single and living alone. He never told me anything about being in a relationship."

"I know what he told you Katy" I felt sorry for this woman, whoever she was, "I've seen all the texts. He was just lining you up while he's been trying to get rid of me. Don't let me get in your way Katy, you're welcome to him but I suspect you might be real sorry within a month from now.

He has succeeded in utterly destroying my life. But who knows? You see, I'm just his nigger whore." Another sob escaped as I said it.

I was about to hang up when I heard her mumble something.

"What was that?" I demanded.

"I said I'm sorry." Now she was crying. "I was introduced to him through his co-workers. They all told me he was single. I would never have let things get to where they are if I'd known. I'll stay well away from him, I promise." She sounded genuinely distressed.

"Don't do that on my account Katy." I had given up on controlling my emotions and it came out in a whining sob. "Do it for yourself. He is one prize con artist with a short attention span and some serious issues."

"Thank you" she said it in a small defeated voice filled with tears. "Thank you for doing what you've done. I owe you"

I cut the call and threw the phone back on the counter.

I went to the bedroom I shared with Samantha and pulled down the two suitcases we had brought our clothes in and started to pack. I had no idea where I was going, but knew I needed to get out of that house. Every moment I was in it made me feel dirtier. The torment and sense of loathing was threatening my sanity.

My cousin Anthony in New York had offered me a room any time I needed it. He was referring more to if I was visiting, but I was sure the invitation would be extended to help out with my present dilemma. He was in the Bronx, an area I knew well but that would mean Samantha having to change schools which would further disrupt her wellbeing. School and the friends she mixed

CHAPTER 12

with there were the only stable aspects of her life as things stood. I couldn't take that away from her as well. Besides if I were to tell Anthony of my problems, and what had brought them about, there was always the possibility he'd get himself in trouble by coming to New Jersey and beating Rob to within an inch of his life. If anyone was going to do that, I wanted it to be me. The news would also spread to St. Lucia via Anthony and I knew how worried Mom would be if she knew how unsettled my life had become and what I was going through. That was just not something I was ready to face.

There was only one option open to me. I picked up the phone and called Peter. It was the hardest thing for me to do. I'd not asked him for anything since our separation, but I had no choice and no-one else to turn to.

When he picked up I almost backed down and a long silence ensued.

"Peter," I finally found my voice. "I have to ask you a huge favor. It's for Samantha."

"You and Rob are separating and you have nowhere to go" he said pre-empting me.

I felt so embarrassed it took me a while to answer. "You're a mind reader." I said eventually.

"No, I'm just not blind. I could see exactly what was happening when you were here this afternoon. Anyone watching would have seen it.... Look I know what's coming Sal, but I work nights. There is nobody here at night, and during the day I sleep and when I'm not doing that I am frequently out pursuing other interests. If Samantha were to come and live here, you would have to come with her. I cannot afford to employ child care." He had it all worked out. Perhaps he'd been talking to Samantha and she'd given him a rundown of our living conditions, or perhaps it had been his perception that forewarned him of my call.

I was devastated. The last thing I needed was to go back to living with Peter. We'd been separated for 6 years, and having to live under his roof again as a house guest would just add to the torment of my dysfunctional life. I had to tally up my choices. There weren't many. I either stayed in Rob's house or moved in with Peter. Which was the lesser of the two evils?... The debate in my head didn't last long. "Can I bring our stuff over tomorrow?"

"Samantha's already here, just bring her clothes and yourself and we'll work it out….. And Sal, this is not a permanent arrangement, you do know that don't you?.... I'm single, I have a life and I'm not going to stop living it. You must get your act together as quickly as possible. "

I understood that to mean he had other women in his life and he didn't want my presence to intervene or disrupt that… "Fine!!" I cut the call and sat down on the bed. I began to cry again. What had I done to deserve what was happening to me? How had my life spiraled so spectacularly out of control? How had I been so totally taken in by Rob? What warning signals had I missed? It had seemed like a match made in heaven and then WHAM!! I thought of Samantha. The guilt over taking her away from our contented settled life to move in with this creature added fuel to the fire of misery burning within me.

I knelt down beside the bed, bowed my head and through the torment and the tears, I began to pray.

"Please God, guide me from this hell. Show me the light to follow so I can find contentment and security for my precious Samantha. Guide me to where I can do an

CHAPTER 12

honest day's work for an honest wage, enough to feed and shelter us. Please God, I beg you as your humble servant show me the way. Amen"

I got up and carried on packing.

"YOU FUCKING BITCH." Rob was in the kitchen, his screamed profanity echoing off the walls through the entire house. I heard him coming towards the bedroom and turned to face him as he walked in the door. "Who the fuck do you think you are to read the messages on my phone? What makes you think you can trespass in my house and invade my privacy you black bitch?"

I stood my ground and stared at him. I was ready to defend myself. If necessary I would bite and kick and scratch and scream. If he came any closer I was going to do whatever I had to do to both defend myself and to physically hurt him as much as I could.

"You shouldn't leave your girlfriend's messages open on the counter for everyone to see Rob. That way, maybe your precious privacy would be protected. I have no interest in your sleazy little affairs and I have no interest in you. Right now you're in my space so get out."

He stood and stared at me in astonishment. He looked confused as he took in the suitcases, the open cupboard and the clothing I had already packed. He was so stoned it took him a few moments to comprehend the significance of the scene.

"Where the fuck do you think you're going?" he sneered.

"You don't have to know that, other than the fact I'm getting as far away from you, your stinking house and your disease ridden mind and body as I can. You disgust me Rob, do you know that. You make my skin crawl."

He suddenly lunged at me, pushing me off balance and

I fell to the floor. He grabbed the suitcase I had almost finished packing and, holding the lid closed, lurched out of the room.

"You're not going anywhere until you pay me the rent you owe me bitch"

I got up from where I had fallen and chased after him. Encumbered by the suitcase he was slow and I had no difficulty catching up with him and I shoved him in the back with all the strength I could muster. He stumbled forward, trying to his hold his balance while keeping a grip on the suitcase. He didn't succeed and fell, dropping the case to break his fall. I got between him and the abandoned case and unleashed an almighty kick into his groin. He screamed as the kick struck home and I felt a rush of adrenaline through my veins, setting me on edge, emboldening me. Suddenly I was not afraid. Suddenly I was in charge; I had the upper hand. The sharp primitive instinct of conquest and survival was upon me and I pounced. All the suppressed frustration and abuse, the humiliation and the insults, the torment and the pain rose from their hiding places within me and rushed out in a combined powerful and determined force of fury, turning me into a monster. Blinded by my anger, I let loose on the writhing wretch at my feet and kicked and punched at every exposed part of his body. I put kick after kick into his groin and it felt amazing. It filled me with a sense of satisfaction I had never felt before. The man I thought I had loved with every cell of my being had turned me into a wild animal and the urge to kill him as he lay there screaming and begging for me to stop, was almost overwhelming. I got a grip of myself and stood over the squirming, pathetic excuse for a man. I was panting as if having run a long way.

CHAPTER 12

"If you ever come anywhere near me or anyone close to me ever again Rob, I swear by all that is holy, I will kill you."... It wasn't me talking... It was something inside of me I had never known existed. Something frightening and ruthless.

I picked up the suitcase and went back into the bedroom and locked the door. As the adrenaline come down kicked in I began to tremble uncontrollably, perspiration sprang from my pores trickling down my neck, back and abdomen, soaking my blouse and jeans. Nausea rose in my throat threatening to explode in a torrent of projectile vomiting. My legs felt as though they might not hold me and I sat down on the bed. Then the tears came again and I wept. I wept in shuddering gulps of anguish and uncertainty as my mind and body fought against the alien instinct of insanity. I had never so much as raised an angry hand to another human in all my life and yet this man had almost driven me to the point of murder. I had used my good foot to kick him as many times as I could and my fists against his head and face. I had no idea how many times I'd struck him or how much damage I'd done. I suddenly became aware of broken skin on my knuckles, and blood on my hands. I held them out, reaching upwards and gave myself to God. With the blood of my conquest over Rob dripping off my hands, I asked God to take me into his care. Samantha was with Peter, she would be alright. I was unsure if I could face another day of being beholden to the patronizing terms of other people for my survival.

Another night without sleep. Another night of anxiety and misgivings. Guilt and sadness consumed me and the tears were relentless. I was being torn apart from the inside and my ability to withstand the continued onslaught of mental anguish was in doubt.

The burden of my circumstances gripped like a vice, squeezing the very substance from my soul. For the first time, the thought of suicide crossed my mind.

Chapter 13

I HAD CLEARED our cupboards and filled the suitcases with our possessions. I looked around the small room to see if I had missed anything, realizing our entire lives were packed into those two cases. That was all we had. My adventure into love had once again stripped me of my dignity and my security. It was 4.30 a.m. and I wanted to be gone from this place. I hoped I would not encounter Rob. I never wanted to see him again, much less talk to him, especially after the violent events of the previous evening. I crept along the passage, through the lounge and to the front door. There was no sign of him. I opened the door and stepped out into the early morning cold. I was half expecting my car to have been vandalized in the night. There was nothing I wouldn't put passed Rob, so I was relieved to find it in one piece with all four tires inflated and no shattered windows, dents or fresh scratches on the bodywork. I placed the cases in the trunk, got in behind the wheel and drove away. I didn't look back.

    I drove the few miles to Peter's house and parked outside. It was still dark and a light snow had settled on the ground. It was too early to knock on the door so I sat in the car, spiritually crushed and mentally frail. It was as if I had toured a full circle. The previous time Peter and I had slept in the same house was on Samantha's 4th birthday, the night he had slept on the couch while I wept bitterly behind our locked bedroom door. The night the true meaning of heartbreak had become clear to me. Now, 6 years later to the day, here I was again, outside his house waiting to be let in under humiliating emotional circumstances. It was as if my spirit had departed, leaving behind an empty shell consumed with self pity, shame and uncertainty. I wondered if it was possible to run out of tears or if I would ever be able to laugh again. Right then neither seemed possible. I turned my head upward and pleaded with God "If you can see me, please show me the way." Suddenly I was overcome with exhaustion and within moments was fast asleep.

I was awakened by Peter tapping on my window. It took me a moment to realise where I was, then rolled the window down.

"There's a bed inside you know, I'm sure it would be more comfortable than the front seat of your car." He was wrapped in an overcoat over his pajamas.

I checked my watch, it was 7.15am. Still dark and cold. Oh so appropriate

"I didn't want to wake you" I said. "And there's nowhere else I can go, so this seemed the most sensible place to wait."

He helped me out of the car and together we carried the bags inside.

"If I may say so," he said kindly as we set the cases down in the hall, "you look terrible. Are you okay?"

"No Peter I'm not. I'm on the verge of a total breakdown. I feel as though my life has been stolen and I'll never get it back." The emotion rose in my throat as I sat on his sofa and the tears flowed without respite.

"Do you want to talk about it?" Peter's voice was soft and compassionate. The voice of a friend, there to lend a sympathetic ear. I knew I was a wreck but the one thing I could count on, certainly for now, my daughter was safe and she could be herself without anxiety. Peter had remained a good father despite our breakup. At least she could sleep without being scared and that gave me a measure of comfort.

"This is a tough situation Peter, and I have no idea how I'm going to cope. I was so happy and secure up until September. Since then it's as if destiny has caught up with me for reasons I don't even understand and I'm being punished for something I know nothing about. What do I do?"

"Get it off your chest as a start. I'm listening. Would you like a coffee?"

He brought the coffee and I poured out my story. Peter had known about Rob right from the beginning and had wished me well. He had done nothing to stand in my way when the relationship blossomed and seemed genuinely pleased for me when he saw how happy I was just before our trip to St. Lucia.

I told him of how a sudden change had come over Rob when we got back from Canada and how insensitive he had been towards me after my surgery and the continuous unpleasantness. I went on to tell him how I found out about his use of cocaine and the complete personality transformation I had witnessed. How he had treated us like unwelcome guests and threatened to have us evicted as trespassers, and the unbearable pressure of being subjected to constant verbal abuse and tension. I ended by telling him of the sms's from Katy, which prompted my call to him, and I told him how I had taken advantage of Rob's condition and half killed him in blind rage.

"And now I'm here." I had shared the torment of my time under Rob's roof and the telling of it had eased the burden. I had stopped crying, though my eyes felt swollen and my heart heavy.

"We need to get you sorted out Sal. You need to find a job and get your self-respect back. You can't go on like this." He was telling me what I had been telling myself for three months. So far nothing had worked.

Peter offered me food. It looked good but I had no appetite. Every time I put food in my mouth, it came straight back up. I drank a lot of water because I was constantly thirsty but was losing weight and looking malnourished. I was in a place I didn't know how to get back from and I knew Peter was doing me a big favour but he really didn't want me there. I didn't know how long I could stay.

Chapter 14

TWO THINGS HAPPENED in quite quick succession and although I didn't realise it then, in hindsight, I now know it was God's hand at work.

Roe Roe, a friend I'd made when I first moved to New Jersey called and invited me for coffee. We'd stayed in touch, but I hadn't seen her for months and this was just a random thought on her part. She had no idea of what had been happening in my life. I was hesitant about going, but knew I needed the company and the fresh air.

When she saw me, she couldn't conceal her surprise. It was obvious my appearance shocked her. I had lost weight and must have looked awful. "You look like a gal with a story to tell" she said as we hugged and took a seat at a terrace table. I looked at her and just couldn't hold it. The tears surfaced again, and then the story of my life over the past 6 months poured out. I stared at my untouched coffee. If I could find the courage to drink the stuff it might help, but I was worried about throwing up. We sat in silence, Roe Roe aghast and I staring down at the table.

"Look, Sall..."

"Uh?" I looked up at her, and fought a war with myself as I knew she was going to give me advice.

"There's a better way to do this. There has to be."

I shrugged. I didn't know what she meant, but it gave me hope. I allowed a little light to navigate the way through the fog that relentlessly obstructed my thoughts. I looked up

Roe Roe said "Anyone can see you are dangerously depressed. You have good reason to be. I'd hazard a guess it's already caused you a nervous breakdown without you recognizing the symptoms. Some people would say you need to visit a psychiatrist, but that is not going to help. I'll tell you what will help, and that is deep meditation through yoga. It will help you rediscover peace of mind and that's where you need to start. You'll sleep better and slowly but surely you'll start to feel yourself again. Some of the studios are pretty expensive, but there are free ones."

When I got back to Peter's house, he was asleep and Samantha was at school. I opened my tablet and searched online for yoga studios. None of those I looked at gave free classes. Far from it, the studios I looked at were way off the charts on charges. While searching, I found the name of an instructor I knew. Karyn had been one of the Friday night friends who joined in with the group I had been part of when I met Rob. I'd known she did yoga and she was very fit, but had never allowed myself to ponder too deeply what it meant.

Karyn worked at a studio in Springfield New Jersey. I reached out to her on the company's site. I told her who I was and she invited me over for an assessment session. We set a time for the following day.

When I arrived Karyn didn't even try to hide her shock at seeing me. "Sally" she said "what happened to you girl?" She hugged me tight and I broke down in her arms. It took me a while to compose myself and she sat patiently looking at me. I repeated the story I had told Roe Roe the day before, and she was horrified at the way Rob had treated me. She had known Rob long before I met him and said she knew he had a drug problem since 2005, but thought he had stopped. I began to cry again and she didn't try to stop me. Finally, as I wiped my eyes, apologizing through sniffles and hiccups she put an arm around me.

"Today is a new beginning for you Sal. You will start fresh and in six months from now you will be healed. You'll be back to sleeping well and your confidence will grow. Everyone needs proper sleep and it's bad enough you aren't eating you need to sleep. I'll put you on a yoga course for depression and anxiety."

I'd never known such a thing existed but I figured Karyn knew what she was doing. I was willing to do anything to get out of this mind frame. She shared an hour of yoga with me for free and provided me with a link to an online free yoga instruction course for both Samantha and I. Since I wasn't working we would be able to do it together in the afternoons when she came home from school. We started doing yoga together twice a week and I did it every day with the link the Karyn had given me.

The other thing I found on the day of my introduction to yoga was quite uncanny. I was waiting for Samantha to arrive home from school and browsing the jobs and agency sites on my tablet when I noticed a sub heading in the side bar with the simple wording, "Come to Jesus." My curiosity aroused, I clicked on it and was guided to a site offering peace of mind and sanctuary in the hands of Jesus Christ. *"Come join in the discussion"* was a slogan beneath the gilded lettering of the site name.

I clicked on the link and was offered the standard "Log

In" or "Register" tags. I was about to back out of it when I decided to take a closer look. I clicked on "Register," typed in my email address, chose a password, confirmed I was not a robot and was prompted to go back to my email and click on the link to verify my bona fides. Finally I was in, and was welcomed to a colourful website proclaiming "Take God into your life, through the hands of Jesus Christ." There was a beautiful image of the Messiah with his hands outstretched and an invitation to "Place your troubles here." I remember thinking to myself in silent prayer, 'Oh God, is it really that easy?' I followed the instructions to 'complete my profile' and once that was confirmed I surfed the options offered in bar tags across the top of the home page and clicked on "Chat."

The chat room seemed like a busy place with dozens of profiles interacting on subjects from the interpretation of Biblical quotes to an atheist searching for a reason to believe in "all this rubbish"

Then I saw my name come up on the screen… "Welcome to our new member Sally. Come share in the glory of God. You're in good company." The message was from someone called Donavan

I typed back "Thank you. God and I are trying to get to know one another"

"No, that's not quite true. God knows you. (he put in a smiley face). God knows everything about you. What you mean, is that you're trying to get to know God?"

"I guess you could say that."

We exchanged a few more messages. He was from Michigan and lived near Lake Eirie. He described the beauty of the area and I was impressed by the way he painted pictures with his words, always praising the glory of God.

CHAPTER 14

He almost had me smiling again. Samantha came home and I thanked Donovan for the chat and said maybe we could catch up another time. He told me he spent a lot of time on the site spreading the word of God, so it was entirely possible we would be on at the same time if I became a regular.

Becoming a chat buddy with someone from Michigan hadn't been part of my curiosity. In my frame of mind, becoming a chat buddy with anyone had its challenges.

"Yeah, sure" I typed "We'll catch up. Bye"

Later, after Samantha has gone to bed and Peter had left for work, I sat alone with myself. It had been a while since I had done anything else in the evening. I thought about the Yoga lessons and about living in Peter's house and about what more I could do to find a job and about Samantha and about a million other things. My mind was a turmoil of incoherent thoughts that seemed to stop short of their destination. I subconsciously associated it with a railway station with multitudes of people in a hurry coming and going in seemingly aimless activity, disappearing to destinations you never see. I was quite lost in every conceivable way.

As if being guided to do so, I reached for my tablet and logged on to the site I'd been in earlier. I entered the 'chat room' and watched the comments appearing on the screen. There were a lot more people online than there had been earlier and among them was Donovan's name. I clicked on it and typed "Hi, I'm back"

"Hi Sally, welcome." The reply was immediate.

We exchanged a few messages, he sounded genuinely interested in hearing what had brought me to the site. "People usually find their way here when hope seems to have abandoned them"

"You don't even scratch the surface" I responded.

"You want to talk about it?"…Who was this stranger wanting me to open my soul… I'd never heard of him and had absolutely no idea if he was even a real person

"Not really. Not now anyway"

"Okay. Nobody's pushing you. You have problems, we listen. It's all up to you. God knows what you're going through, whatever it is. He brought you to it, He'll bring you through it, we just try to help the process along."

"Who's 'we' ?"

"The site admin. We're a group of volunteers. God's hand guided us to set this site up. I honestly believe we've helped a lot of people. Some stay the distance, some don't. There's no pressure, nobody's in a hurry….. except some of the people reaching out. We help where we can."

Donovan started asking me questions I was reluctant to answer, but he made me feel he knew what I was going through. There was a private message facility a click away on the site, and he suggested we move off the main page. He seemed to understand the uncertainty and insecurity of how day to day existence played on a person's self respect and stripped one of dignity. Perhaps it was my need to talk, perhaps it was the gentle way he described things and how he framed the questions he asked, but I found myself pouring my heart out to this stranger. I told him of my relationship with Rob, I told him how much I had believed in him in the beginning and how he had so suddenly changed. I told him how secure and content I had been and how much I'd given up, without even realizing it, to be with Rob and how my faith in the future with him had been rewarded with the destruction of my self esteem. I told him of the arrangement I had with Peter and how it was unlikely to work for any length of time.

Chatting online just about every evening became a source of inspiration and his encouragement plus my daily yoga sessions started to make a difference. The constant state of depression and anxiety I had suffered from were easing and I found myself looking forward to the exchanges. He was far enough away for a face to face meeting to be out of the questions, yet he was close enough via our online chats to be a mentor.

After about 10 days of exchanging typed messages, he asked me if I would like to chat voice to voice over the phone. I was hesitant but thought 'what the heck.' I had confided so much anyway and come away feeling better, it wasn't going to make any difference. I gave him my phone number.

I am convinced Donovan was sent by God at a time I needed someone the most. He was kind and understanding and spoke with the confidence of a true counselor. He encouraged me in a kind softly spoken way that helped me relax and literally breathe out the contamination within me. We spoke of my difficulty in finding a job and he asked to see my resume which I emailed to him. After he had gone through it he replied to my mail telling me it needed work. "We can give it a far more professional touch" he wrote. "Give me a few days with this and I'll fix it so there will be no doubt about your ability and suitability."

I gave him few days and what he sent back was very impressive. Without changing anything fundamental, he had given it a whole new, far more attractive and professional appearance. Every day we either spoke or chatted online. He was kindhearted and had a calming effect on me. He had obviously had some kind of training as he seemed to know how fragile I was and always said the right things to lift my spirits. He encouraged me constantly and made me promise to apply for ten jobs a day. He offered to prepare me for interviews when I got replies. I could feel the difference he was making to my disturbed and delicate frame of mind. I started to feel strength of spirit taking hold and my self esteem returning. Each time I got a rejection to a job I had applied for, he would calm me down. "That's not the one God wanted for you." He'd say. "Something better will come up." I thanked God for sending this patient man my way.

Finally one day in June 2016 I got a job interview with a prominent government department and I came away feeling it had gone very well. Two days later, they called and made me an offer and said I could start at the beginning of July. I had no hesitation in accepting it. It wasn't perfect, but it was a job and my first step towards reclaiming my life.

I called Don and he sounded as excited as I was. He made me feel as though I had achieved something against big odds and showered congratulations on me. Then we prayed together and I praised God with gratitude. I felt as though some light was finally shining.

The yoga was strengthening my body and my mind. The anxiety and depression were receding and I was starting to feel I was regaining my self-respect. After our evening yoga sessions I would lay down and my brain was at peace. I was able to fall asleep and sleep right through the night.

Even if I got up to use the bathroom I'd go straight back to sleep. Yoga is a very powerful healer and the meditation is awesome. When the fear of Rob or anything else in my life caused me anxiety I could breathe it away. Inhale relaxation and tranquility, exhale tension and anxiety.

Chapter 15

JULY 5TH 2016, I walked into work at the government office. I was so honored and felt deep down this job would be part of rebuilding my confidence. With the help of the power of God and my hero Donovan I was getting back to the positive person I had been before meeting Rob.

Going to work and meeting new people, getting up in the morning with a purpose and earning a wage gave everything around me a brighter appearance and I was smiling again. The one constant drag on my conscience and on my sense of contentment was having to live in Peter's house. It made me uncomfortable despite the fact we hardly saw each other. His night shift had him leaving for work before 5.00 pm and I usually hadn't surfaced by the time he got home at around 5.30am. The arrangement was tolerable, but Samantha and I were living as guests in his house, presenting a constant source of frustration. We needed a place we could call our own. Peter wasn't used to having full time house guests and it showed in silly but obvious ways. He was an atheist. He'd always been an atheist and in the years we had lived together and been married that had never worried or concerned me. Now, when I told him I had God and the Lord Jesus in my life, he ridiculed my belief which set me on edge but I let it go. On the occasions we were all in the house at the same time the atmosphere was never completely relaxed. Peter had suggested I save all my wages for 6 months to provide me with a fund I could draw on to get established in an apartment of our own. That sort of suggested he was giving us a deadline of 6 months and he would support us but it didn't provide me with any sense of relief. I didn't want to be there any more than he wanted us there.

 Without warning, it came to a head. It was a little over 3 months since we'd moved in when I go a text message from Peter at work. Very brief, it just said "We need to talk, I'm off tonight, what time will you be home?" I text back, "I'll be there by six", and thought no more of it..

 I was so unprepared for what he had to say, it stripped me of all the confidence I had gained over the months.

 "Sal, I want you to find a room of your own to live in. You can leave Samantha with me. I'll carry on paying you the child support to help you along, then once you're back on your feet we'll revisit the situation, but this arrangement isn't working. "

 I looked at him in disbelief. It took a while to sink in. He was actually kicking me out and I had nowhere to go. "You gave us 6 months Pete. You said for me to save my wages for 6 months, we've only been here 3. You can't do this to us Pete." I was devastated and more than a little desperate. What we had was far from ideal, but it provided a roof over our heads and a place to sleep. A shadow of fear rose in my stomach.

 "I'm not talking about Samantha leaving," He seemed

quite calm and sure of himself. There was no outward indication of guilt or shame, "I said you should leave Samantha with me and we'd take another look at the arrangement once you're in a position to cope."

"I'm not leaving my daughter anywhere Peter, if I go she comes with me." Now I was angry. How could he do this and why? "Why are you doing this Pete? I know it's not the best of circumstances, but I've not been in your way and I contribute. What has brought about this sudden change of heart?" I felt as though I was begging. It was humiliating and I was cast back into a state of anxiety I had not felt since leaving Rob. My emotions were in a tangle and tears had flooded my eyes.. "Why Peter? You know it's not as easy as walking out the door and into alternative accommodation."

"I'm not putting you on the street Sally, I'm putting you on notice to find another place. It's not working with you here and all that religious shit."

I ignored his last remark. "I'm not leaving Samantha here Peter, just get that into your head. If I go, she goes. Don't forget how you fixed it to minimize your responsibility 6 years ago. I have custody and I will shoulder that responsibility no matter what it takes."

"In your circumstances, you may have some difficulty convincing a custody review panel of your suitability to retain custody." He was so cold and calculating it made me want to lash out at him. The memory of how ugly he had been over the divorce had faded, but now came rushing back. I knew he was capable of extreme malice,

"Why are you doing this Peter?" I was crying openly now. "What have I done that you're being like this?"

He looked me in the eye and said very simply "I'm

seeing a few female friends. I'm having sex with all of them. I'm not going to check into motels when I have a perfectly good home I can bring them to. I need sex and I'm not going to change my life for you, so I've come to the conclusion you have to go."

I would have applauded him on his virility if I'd been given time to think, but his frankness caught me flat footed and I was lost for words. His revelation added to my sense of incredulity. The subject of sex hadn't so much as entered my head for months and now my ex-husband was throwing me out of his home so he could indulge his desires with other women. It took me a full minute to absorb that. Nothing was of less interest to me than how Peter spent his spare time. The fact he had a harem of women coming and going solicited no more significance for me than if he had taken to stamp collecting. The fact I was being evicted to facilitate his promiscuous lifestyle left an unpleasant taste in my mouth. For reasons I did not fully comprehend, I would have preferred it had he given me another reason, but it did give my argument a lifeline.

"So you're throwing me out to make way for a bus load of sluts coming through here, and you want me to leave my daughter behind to witness it?... Have you lost your mind?"

I could feel the strength of my resolve rising and flexing its muscles. I wasn't going to back down on this. "You can live any kind of life you want to Peter, you've always done that anyway. But if you think a custody review will stand up to scrutiny under the circumstance you've just presented, then your brains have slipped into your groin. Give me a week to find a place and we'll leave. You don't have to change anything for us, and besides I want a Christian upbringing for Samantha, you would crush her faith in God. " I glared at him then turned and walked away.

The bravado and bluster had emerged from that reserve of God given inner strength and pride. I had no idea if we would find somewhere to live within a week; in fact I had serious doubts. I couldn't take time off work and the money I had put aside was never going to be enough for the deposit on a tent much less a place where Samantha could do homework and sleep comfortably.

I went to my room and to my horror Samantha was standing just inside the door with tears in her eyes. I thought to myself God why me? God I need you. Guide me oh Lord.

I took Samantha in my arms and held her tight. She looked at me through her tear filled eyes. "Mommy I don't want you to lose me or me lose you."

I hugged her and said "I'm not going anywhere without you my darling. God will make a way." I had to keep my own emotions in check. The tears were not far from the surface.

The last thing I needed for my child was more anxiety. She had suffered enough through the torment of our insecurity. I tried to think of who we could call on for help without disrupting Samantha's schooling. Donovan had become such a reliable friend, but he was in Michigan 820 miles away. There wasn't much he could do apart from listen and calm me down. He was good at that.

We ate dinner in silence and then Peter went out. As soon as I heard him drive away, I called Donovan.

"Hi there friend" His greeting was always bright and cheerful. I could hear the laughter in his voice, light and uplifting. A far cry from the way I felt.

"I have a big problem Don." I was barely able to keep my voice steady. Anxiety sat in my abdomen like a lump of toxic dough and the indignity of being nothing more than an expendable entity in the lives of others ate away my self-respect. I told him about my "meeting" with Peter and what had come out. "I'm back to where I started." I was sobbing again. I was being crushed underfoot by circumstances again.

"God works in mysterious ways Sal." He sounded so calm, so unflustered and reasonable it was like a stimulant for me. "There is a bigger plan for you and it can't be realized while you're in Peter's house."

"It can't be realized while I'm walking the streets homeless either Don."

"Well you won't know until you know. Let's make sure you don't become homeless, just hang in there it will all work out. Keep looking for apartments and I'll look for you as well."

"How are you going to help Don? You're in Michigan, I'm in New Jersey!"

"I'll send you some accommodation links, go check them out. If all else fails, there are always homeless shelters."

The thought terrified me. It was the last place I wanted to end up. It was like a shelter for the homeless and I couldn't believe Don would suggest it.

"Maybe God wants you to be a messenger for the homeless and Godless?" he said, "Like Jonah in the Bible. He didn't want to go either but it was God's calling. But hey, don't despair, we'll get you sorted into accommodation, you'll see."

Going to a shelter wasn't *MY* calling. I was going to

fight with every fiber of my being to make sure that didn't happen.

I had been feeling so much better about myself. The deep depression I'd been suffering from had receded and with Don's help and the Yoga sessions, life had been much brighter despite the imperfect situation of living in Peter's house. Now I was feeling very fragile again. What had I done to deserve everything that had happened to me. What was God's purpose of taking me away from my contented, secure life to go off and take up with a schizophrenic loser like Rob? It just seemed so unfair and I was so emotionally ill equipped to deal with the consequences. The familiar weighty force of depression was once again bearing down on me and my ability to withstand it again was perilously in doubt.

To add to my plight, there were problems at work as well. A personality clash between me and one of my co-workers was creating tension in the office. Being new at the job, I had a lot to learn. That was clearly understood at my interview, but this woman tried everything in her power to make me feel out of place and did nothing to help me when I needed it. She made a habit of passing scathing remarks about how unhealthy I looked, how thin I was and made a point trying to humiliate me in front of other co-workers. I had tried to ignore her, but it hadn't helped and nobody was coming to my defence. On one occasion I had ended up in a toilet cubicle with tears of anger and frustration streaming down my face, desperately trying to prevent my sobs from being heard in the washstand area. A week earlier I had reported the woman to our department manager, but he didn't show any interest. He said harmless banter between the staff was part of working there. I should cheer up and be more part of the team. When I explained I was being shunned and not made to feel welcome as "part of the team", he said I shouldn't be so sensitive. He was clearly not going to intervene, so I had taken my grievance to Human Resources. As it turned out that wasn't a great career enhancing maneuver. The manager took the side of my nemesis and the Human Resources mentor was reluctant to take any action and the harassment continued. My position at work was almost as precarious as my accommodation woes.

I prayed to God, begging Him to show me the way, show me the light to follow, let this torment end. It was almost a year since I had met Rob. A year in time, starting with what I had mistaken for love and deliverance from a mundane existence but had turned out to be one of the worst errors of judgment I had ever made. It was ten months since we had embarked on our trip to St. Lucia which was the last time I had been truly happy. A whirl of ecstasy and passion, riding the wave of euphoria before being dumped unceremoniously on the beach of shattered dreams. Why me? Why me Lord?

Donovan was my pillar of strength. Each day he sent me inspirational videos, willing me to stay strong and adding his personal messages "C'mon.., you can beat this." "C'mon, you're stronger than you think." When I was ready to give up on myself, Donovan would be there to lift my spirits. "Winners don't quit"… "C'mon Sally, weakness is voluntary, so is strength, put on a positive attitude."

Time was running out, and in spite of Donovan's encouragement I was no closer to finding a place for Samantha and I to move into. I prayed constantly. I prayed while I was working, I prayed on the bus to and from work and I knelt down beside my bed every night begging for a miracle. I had put my name down with so many rental agencies, hoping to find a home in a good neighborhood, something affordable, but nothing on offer fitted into my budget. In the wake of my altercations at work, there was no chance of early promotion or an increase in wages, and the apartments were all just too expensive.

But I was not going to give up. My goal was to have the keys to our own home and Peter reminded me daily, my time was running out.

Chapter 16

MY DETERMINATION AND my pride clashed. There was no way I was going to ask Peter for an extension of time, and by the end of the week I was no closer to finding a place for us to live. I was left with no choice but to seek shelter for my daughter and I through charitable means and while Peter was at work I packed our bags once again and we left. By the time he discovered we had left, there would be no trace of us ever having been there.

In my mind, there was no choice and at 7.30 in the evening we walked into a shelter in Plainfield New Jersey. There were many other people standing in line and I couldn't bear to think how far we had fallen. There were elderly people in clothing resembling rags. Dirty people with bad breath and pungent body odour, shifty eyes with long, greasy hair, and toothless mouths. Men and women of indiscriminate ages looking like drug users with vacant eyes and "roll your own" cigarettes dangling from their mouths. I had been reduced to joining the rejects and dregs of society. Never, in my worst nightmares would I have imagined ending up with my daughter in a place like this. It was like being in prison and I had no idea what crime I had committed. The sense of humiliation and shame taking Samantha to that place caused an emotional cocktail of desperation to well up within me, and the weight of despair seized at me like a clamp.

When we reached the front of the line the woman behind the desk looked at us with skepticism. She cast her eyes over our two suitcases. Other people had their possession confined to one or two plastic shopping bags. She was a large, harsh looking woman with a slit for a mouth and graying hair rolled into a bun on top of her head. She wore a grey house coat and her bi-focal spectacles perched on the end of her nose.

"What do you want?" she barked, and without waiting for an answer went on "Been thrown out by the husband?.. You a hooker on the run from your pimp?.. We don't want no trouble in here. You a hooker you get back on the street and keep your trouble away from here."

"Just like all these people," I cast my hand is a sweeping gesture taking in the homeless standing in line or lounging against the faded walls, "I'm homeless and I need shelter for my daughter and me. We won't be staying long." I said it with as much humility as I felt.

"You looking to get robbed coming in here all dressed up to the nines." Our clothes were like Gucci when compared to the dress of the others. "Don't you come complaining when all your fancy stuff is gone."

She looked down at the papers on her desk, and without looking at me scribbled something on a printed form. "Name?" I wasn't prepared for the question and didn't hear her properly.

"I beg your pardon?"

"Your name,.. what's your name girl?" She made it sound like I was being interrogated. I gave it to her. "Social security number?".. I recited the number.. "And the kid?"

she pointed the back of her pen in Samantha's direction. I gave her Samantha's name. She scrawled our details on the form then tore off a perforated section at the bottom and pushed it across to me. "Dormitory 5 on the first floor. Be gone by 6.30am and don't smoke.. Next."

We found dormitory 5 and I cringed. It was a long narrow room with dirty windows and faded paint peeling from the walls. Narrow iron framed beds with lumpy mattresses and one folded thread bear blanket on each lined the walls on either side. The room was almost full to capacity with women looking like bag ladies. Straggly, unwashed hair over faces bearing the blemishes of too much alcohol and nicotine. Most of them wore clothing that hadn't been washed in weeks and despite the warning of "Don't smoke," there was the stench of stale tobacco in the air mingling with the odour of unwashed bodies.

We commandeered two bunks side by side in the far corner and I pushed our suitcases as far under the bed as they would go. I was trying to be brave for Samantha and held back the volcano of tears and despair bubbling just below the surface of my resolve. She looked quite bewildered and I had no words of comfort for her. We couldn't stay there. I thought of leaving right then and taking Samantha back to Peter's house, then going somewhere quiet and peaceful where I could destroy myself and be free from the constant weight of guilt and anguish. The idea was becoming more and more appealing but all the time, through the pain of humiliation and torment I felt the tug of God's presence. He was preparing me for something else. Something important.....*Breathe!! Inhale relaxation and tranquility, exhale tension and anxiety.* I sat on the narrow bunk in the dormitory for homeless people and crossed my legs. Adopting my yoga position I closed my eyes and blew out the bad spirits infesting me. I didn't care who was watching.

I didn't sleep and the night dragged by. Sounds of loose phlegm coughing, sleep talkers and deep throat snoring would have kept me awake even if sleep had been trying to claim me. It was sometime around 11.30pm a figure appeared at the open door and swept a flashlight over the sleeping forms in the beds. The beam floated towards me and I lay still with my eyes closed. The figure appeared to be that of a man although I couldn't be sure, and it lingered for a while before moving away. I wondered why a man would be wandering around the women's sleeping quarters at that time of night. It seemed ominous and added to my sense of insecurity and confinement. It made me think of a prison warder doing his duty rounds.

As I lay on that uncomfortable bed, I questioned the unfairness of my situation. Not for the first time I saw myself a prisoner of circumstances. I felt God was preparing me for what was ahead, but I felt sure there were other ways to do it. I had committed no crime other than poor judgment. Why am I in prison? Why is my ten years old child in prison with me? The emotions became too much to hold back and tears rolled down my cheeks. I would get through. I was convinced it was all part of the test that God had laid for me.

I woke Samantha at 5.30am and we crept from the dormitory and out through the front door. I couldn't bear to stay in that place for a minute longer. I had to make an alternative arrangement for that night.

We found a nearby all night diner on Park Street off West 7th and ordered breakfast. I left our bags in the car but carried a small toilet bag containing our tooth brushes and a sponge to use in the washroom. It was a futile gesture, but I needed to make an attempt to wash away the sense of dirt I imagined to be clinging to us like an odour. At 7.00am, I dropped Samantha at school and made arrangements to have her stay in the after care center until I came to collect her after work. I had absolutely no idea where we would end up that night.

On the way to work I passed Winnoco Park in Elizabeth and I was completely taken in by an impulse. I parked the car got out and walked out on the green grass and I knelt down with arms opened wide and prayed.

"Please God look upon me your humble servant. Look upon the life of Samantha and guide us. We are lost in a wilderness of uncertainty and scorn. Please dear God show me the way. Lay upon me the mantle you wish me to carry. Expose to me the task for which you have been preparing me and allow me to serve you. We are ready dear God. Show me the light. Amen."

When I got back into the car I phoned Don and told him everything. I needed to offload and I described our first night as homeless people.

As usual, he was sympathetic and supportive. His soft comforting voice immediately gave me hope and helped me feel more confident.

"I have never come across anyone who has endured what you have been through and still remained positive" he said.

"It's not easy Don. There are times when being positive

is just a thought. Finding the strength to match up is not so easy."

"When God is involved anything is possible." He assured me. "When God is for you, who can be against you?"

Having my resolve tested to the extent it was, gave me moments of doubt but I didn't tell Don that. By the time I got to work it felt as though I had already put in a full day and it was only just after 8.00am.

I had tried every rental agency I could find in New Jersey and my name was down with all of them as a candidate to rent accommodation. It was hard to believe, not a single one of those agencies could find me a place to stay and I got on the phone to put pressure on the people I had spoken to. The most common reason I was being overlooked was the size of my budget... "Hell Sally, I could have you in and settled by this afternoon if you could up your offer." Each agent in turn had a similar reason to why they hadn't found me a room to rent. I knew it was true. The rent I could afford was way below the going rate for a half decent place, but I couldn't go any higher.

The harassment I was being subjected to by some of my work colleagues made it awkward for me to ask for a raise or a better position. I was still a learner and didn't want to ruffle any feathers. If I were to lose the job it would mean disaster for us, so I did what was asked of me and kept a low profile. That didn't help my devastating circumstances. I hadn't told anybody at work about my accommodation problems and nobody knew I had been rendered homeless, seeking shelter in places they wouldn't believe existed. Constant anxiety because of our situation drained my confidence and instilled within me a sense of dread. It was like the sensation of sitting at the very edge of a towering

CHAPTER 16

cliff with nothing to hold on to, yet being stuck there and unable to move to safety. My desperation to find security and a normal way of life again was taking its toll on my sanity, I was sure of it. I worked the phones till I had spoken to all the accommodation agents and I was no further forward by the time I was done.

The work on my desk wasn't going away and I needed to get through that. I really didn't want to go back to the shelter that night. I really didn't want to live like this anymore. Sometimes I imagined I could see the angel of death calling me to him with the friendly gesture of a waving arm. Sometimes the temptation to answer the call and follow was almost irresistible. Holding back tears of frustration and misery was an unremitting emotional challenge.

Chapter 17

WE DID END up back at the shelter that night; there was nowhere else to go. I recognized some of the people from the previous night but there were others I'd not seen before. Rag tag souls with defeat hanging onto their shoulders and in their eyes like dead weights. There was a woman with a small baby. I say woman, but she was probably still in her teens, she had multiple piercings in her face (nose, lips, cheeks and eyebrows), and hideous satanic tattoos down both arms. Her hair was cropped short and ragged as if she had done a bad job of shaving it and it was trying to make a comeback. She seemed to cough with every alternate breath. The child was wrapped in a dirty knitted blanket and cried incessantly. It was clearly not well and equally clear the mother hadn't noticed. Holding Samantha's hand, I approached the girl and offered to help pacify the child. She looked at me through vacant eyes and seemed to have difficulty focusing.

"You want the fucking kid?" she finally got her vision in check and spat the question. "You want the fucking kid? Who the fuck do you think you are? Is it your fucking kid?"

Her response was so unexpected I reeled back as if I'd been slapped. "I'm just offering to help. I can see you're under a lot of strain." I was probably under just as much strain, but I wasn't loaded with drugs and a screaming baby. It struck me I was well off by comparison.

"Yeah, well if I need your help I'll let you know, now fuck off."

I wasn't sure if I was embarrassed or angry over the girl's attitude but took Samantha back to our place in the registration line without another word. She looked up at me with tears in her eyes and my heart nearly broke. "She didn't need to be like that mommy. Don't worry; she's got worse troubles than we have." Coming from my ten year old daughter, I felt my heart swell with pride so it rose to my eyes and overflowed down my cheeks. Samantha put her arms around me in a comforting gesture and I thanked God for giving this child to me.

The night passed much like the one before and once again I slept very little. The coughing and snoring in addition to the crying baby didn't help. I had left our cases in the trunk of our car which I had parked two blocks away so as not to attract attention, and I had our toiletries in a shopping bag. We would need to stand in line for a shower. There was no way I could go a second day without cleaning myself properly, especially after two nights on a mattress previously used by any number of lice infested drifters. Even the air in the place made me feel dirty but the showers were only opened at 6.00am. I made sure we were first in the queue by waking Samantha at 5.30 and taking our belongings with us to wait in the dingy corridor outside the ablution rooms.

Showering in communal facilities among the sick and homeless was something I would never have imagined I would be doing. I was not one of these people, I was not a loser. I was an ambitious, hard working and reliable individual. How had I ended up in that situation? As I washed the dirt from my body, I prayed to God to deliver me from this place. Help me find a place where we could be comfortable and secure.

Just after dropping Samantha at school my prayers were answered. While driving to work my mobile rang. The caller ID came up as Ramon. He was a guy from "Home Comforts", one of the agencies I had registered with.

"Hi Sally, how are you?" I had no intention of going into detail of how I was. I was in a place nobody would understand and few would care.

"I am doing alright thanks Ramon. What can you tell me?"

"Did you get a room yet?" I felt my spirits rise, he wouldn't be calling me to exchange small talk.

"Not yet Ramon, I'm living in a shelter for the homeless and I'm desperate, do you have something to help me change that?"

There was a long pause, and then. "You're kidding right? You're not really in a shelter are you?" He sounded incredulous, like he thought I was joking.

"I'm not kidding Ramon, I wish I was. What can you tell me?"

"Well I called to tell you I found a room for you. It's part of a home sharing scheme. You and Samantha will have you own room but all the facilities like bathroom, kitchen dining and living rooms are communal and it fits neatly into your budget."

I thought about that for a moment. It sounded like one peg above the shelter we had been in. Having our own room was a plus, but our privacy would be infringed on all the time. What was I thinking? Where we were, privacy was nonexistent, everything was communal even the toilet cubicles and they didn't even have doors on them.

"Where is it and when can I see it?" Anything had to be better that what we had and I didn't want to spend another night in that dormitory if I didn't absolutely have to.

"The lady's name is Mary. She's a devout Christian so you'll be in good company." I had made a point of telling people of my reliance on God and the spirit of the Lord Jesus.

Immediately I got off the phone with Ramon, I called Mary. She sounded friendly and efficient but abrupt. She quickly extracted all there was to know about me and my daughter. She described the property to me along with the way things worked in a 'shared accommodation environment' before saying, "I think you would fit in here Sally, when do you want to move in?"

I hadn't seen the place, but Mary sounded nice and her description made it sound like unbelievable luxury when compared with the shelter.

"If the room is ready for us Mary, I'd like to move in this afternoon." I had to get Samantha to a place where we could wash our clothes and start to feel human again.

As it turned out, the room was quite small but bright and clean with pretty floral curtains and bed spreads to match. The walls were freshly painted in soft pastel shades and the single window overlooked a small, neatly kept garden. A spacious bathroom with toilet, basin, shower cubicle and bath was at the end of a short passage with dining and kitchen facilities downstairs. Mary was quite the opposite of the mental image I had created during our phone conversation. She was a buxom woman with a harsh disapproving manner who reminded me of the registration desk jockey at the shelter. Her spectacles dangled at the end of a chain around her neck bouncing against her ample bosom as she walked and her dress was a dull high neck frock with puff shoulders. She would have fitted perfectly into a movie role of matron at a nineteenth century school for wayward boys. She was, nonetheless, not unpleasant and once I had paid her she handed me the keys and left me alone to unpack. As soon as I had done that, I rushed off to fetch Samantha from the after care center at school. I couldn't wait to tell her the news that we would not be going back to the shelter that night. All the way in the car, I thanked God for turning up and praised the glory of His divine presence.

I had decided to take Samantha out to eat and not rush to get back. We were no longer governed by a curfew and the idea was as much to celebrate our freedom as it was to spring the surprise on her. I knew she would be so relieved we weren't going back to the shelter and she was. She threw her arms around me when I told her about the room.

"Mommy you are the most wonderful person. Thank you. I really hated it in that dormitory." Her obvious delight almost had me in tears again. We had no way of knowing it then, but our delight and new found freedom was to be short lived.

On the night of our second day at Mary's we were getting ready for bed. Samantha was in the shower and I was at the basin brushing my teeth. Suddenly Samantha let out a scream and simultaneously a surge of water burst from the shower cubicle hitting me in the face. I turned to see water pouring from the wall where the shower head had been. The pipe was broken off flush with the wall and a single jet of water gushed out like a fire hose. I quickly turned off the faucet but the bathroom floor was covered in water.

"What happened?" I asked. Samantha was in tears.

"I just raised my arm to wash and I bumped my hand against the shower head. It just broke off. I'm sorry mommy."

There was no need for her to apologize, it wasn't her fault. Clearly the pipe was corroded and it was just unfortunate that Samantha had been the one to dislodge it. I took her in my arms and pacified her. "It's not a big deal." I assured her. "It can be fixed, and it's not your fault."

We cleaned up the flooded bathroom floor and went in search of Mary to report the broken shower head. At first she was quite calm about it and told me not to worry she would get it fixed but the next day was quite different.

As I was leaving the house the following morning to get Samantha to school and me to work, Mary called out to me. At first I didn't realize she was talking to me, as she called me Molly.

"Molly" she said. "I need to talk to you." Her harsh tone matched the image of the uncompromising hostel matron I had formed the first time I had met her. I immediately sensed trouble. "I can't allow carelessness that causes damage to my property and I need to re-evaluate the terms of our agreement."

I was so unprepared for the aggressive rebuke my defence system took a moment to realise I was under attack. "What are you talking about?" I was still smiling as I said it.

"I don't know what it is about you people, but you seem

to break everything you touch."

I was no longer smiling. "Just define the term *'you people'*" I challenged. "And then tell me what on earth you're talking about." I was not going to be spoken to like that by anyone. I knew exactly what she was getting at. She was referring to people of colour as being destructive and it was her way of confronting a racial issue she had obviously not thought about when accepting me as a tenant over the phone.

"That shower head has been ripped from the wall." She accused. "That was no simple accident." She ignored my challenge on the *'you people'* remark.

By then I was fuming. The altercation had caught me completely by surprise and instinctively I knew it was not going to be resolved. She had not known that Samantha and I were people of colour until I had shown up and it had gone against her expectations. Against her prejudice. She needed an excuse to get us out.

"That shower head was in a condition that was going to cause an accident and potentially serious injury." I didn't know if that was true, but I used it anyway. "The pressure from the water could have blasted that rusted pipe out of the wall and hit someone on the head." Then I let rip at her and I even surprised myself with the strength of my outburst. "You know now, as well as anyone that the next person to touch that shower head was going to break it. The pipe was so rusty I'm surprised it lasted as long as it did. You call yourself a Christian. You call yourself a person of God and yet you allow stupid prejudice and racism to control you. We both know what this is about Mary, and the shower head is just a bi-product, just an excuse for you. You didn't know I was black when we spoke on the phone, but the minute you saw me you needed an excuse for this conversation to go ahead. You're no Christian, you're no person of God, you're just another hypocrite brandishing the Bible to give yourself a sense of credibility. Well, until I see fit to find alternative accommodation, you're stuck with us so get used to it. And by the way, the name is Sally, not Molly. Get used to that as well."

She looked at me as if she had been slapped. In a sense I guess she had been. I walked through the door and slammed it behind me. Samantha had already gone to the car, so thankfully hadn't witnessed the confrontation. I however, was very nervous about what had just occurred.

As expected, from that point on everything was a problem with Mary. She got the shower fixed, but her true colours came out bright and unmistakable. She objected to where I parked my car, she objected if one of us spent too long in the bathroom, she objected to me listening to my radio and if we were watching TV, she would deliberately change the channel. In fact there was nothing she did not object to and the pressure of living there became a lot worse than the undercurrent of pressure that had existed at Peter's house. Once again we were being tested and I needed to find us somewhere else to live. This wasn't working.

Staying calm and convincing myself God was working on our side was becoming more and more difficult to believe.

Speaking to Donovan at least twice a week and sometimes more remained a source of reassurance. He had been thrilled when I'd told him about getting a room at Mary's and was equally disappointed when I broke the news of how it had turned out. But he had been busy on our behalf and had the name of a shelter called Family Promise in Union County, Elizabeth.

"I don't want to go back to a shelter Don." I was quite distraught by the idea "And I definitely don't want Samantha to experience living in a shelter again."

"Sally, go and see them," he urged. "The Union County Program is overseen by the National Family Promise office. It provides a holistic approach through a comprehensive set of services to families experiencing homelessness and families at risk of homelessness in Union County. I've checked them out Sal, and spoken to the case manager. It's not the kind of shelter you've been exposed to. You and Samantha can find your feet again while you're there. It's not the YMCA and from what you tell me, you're not in a good place right now anyway. Go see them, they have space and you can fit into their programme."

Reluctantly I agreed. Somewhere deep within me I felt this might be a stepping stone to freedom and fulfillment and hesitantly called the number Donovan had given me.

The reception I got from the lady who picked up the call was like a ray of sunshine after a long heavy thunder storm. She immediately made me feel as though I was doing the right thing by calling. She had all my details and confirmed she had been the person who Donovan had spoken with.

"We have space for you and your daughter and we want to help. Your friend Donovan explained what a torrid time you've been through and what a strong character you are to have endured so much. God has seen you through the worst; Family Promise will help put you back on your feet."

By the time I got off the phone I already felt like I belonged to the family of promise and I resolved to give Mary notice when I got home that evening. I drafted a letter confirming my intention to leave her toxic house, although I didn't put it quite that way. I simply informed her in writing I had been offered accommodation in an environment more conducive to my Christian values.

Chapter 18

FROM THE MINUTE we arrived at 402 Union Avenue in Elizabeth New Jersey, I sensed I had been guided there by the will of God. The last thing I had wanted was to be confined to another shelter, but this was something I had not expected. In stark contrast to the reception we had received at the YMCA, here were people who made us feel they really cared. Unlike our experience in a crowded dormitory with dirty people in dirty clothes and poor health, we were allocated our own room and although small, it was clean and comfortable. I was inspired by the kindness of the people and believed from the beginning I could help here as well as being a beneficiary. I learned that the insecurity and despair Samantha and I had experienced through our ordeals was not uncommon among the people we were now sharing a home with. If anything, we had come off lightly. We were better off in many ways than most of our fellow travelers. I was able to see how the frustration and hopelessness of our situation was not confined to us, but was a widespread phenomenon. There were mothers with small children bearing the scars of physical abuse by their partners and abandoned women with tiny babies who would have died on the streets if not for the compassion of Family Promise and the kindness of the volunteer staff.

In as much as I didn't want to be in a shelter, I felt it was my calling to be there. This is where God wanted to show me the true meaning of Christian values. Mary had pushed back at me when refunding my deposit. She'd held back seventy dollars and told me it was for the cost of repairing the showerhead. I simply looked at her with pity in my eyes and voice as I said, "You know you don't have the right to do that. The damage was caused by wear and tear, and poor maintenance, not by Samantha. You know it and I know it. But Mary, if it makes you feel good, if it makes you feel like you're doing your Christian duty and upholding your Christian values, keep the seventy dollars. It may be useful when you have to pay the ferryman on your way to hell."

I was almost in tears again as I left. I needed the seventy dollars a whole lot more than she did and it was not her right to keep it. Short of calling the police and creating a massive neighborhood scene, there was nothing I could do about it, so I let it go and left her in the hope she would suffer from a guilty conscience, knowing she had robbed me. In a strange sort of way, it made me feel good. Like I had won.

Family Promise is associated with the Faith Lutheran Church in Scotch Plains New Jersey and we went there frequently. For the first time in months I was starting to meet some really nice, kind people. They gave me an insight into an environment of charity and as time went by, I came to the conclusion I wanted to become part of their community. I realized I wanted to be able to help people who were going through what I had suffered. These people didn't know our history and it didn't seem to matter to them. They gave of themselves in compassion and spiritual kindness and gave dignity to the less fortunate. I still did not want to be in a shelter, I wanted a home of my own to share with Samantha, like it was before… Like it should be, but I could see so many ways I could help in an environment of less privileged people. How I could become a part of other people's healing process while giving strength to my own. I was a nurse, I am a nurse, I just knew, I could learn to nurse the spirit and the soul as well as the body.

Over the weeks and months with Family Promise, it became clear to me why God had made me suffer. I had needed to know what people were going through to be able to understand the role he had mapped out for me. It made me feel so humble because I knew in my heart I'd been selected by God to help others. As I cast my mind back over the months of anguish, humiliation and hardship, things started to make sense. I was able to join the dots and trace a pattern.

I had allowed God to slip out of my life even though Mom had made Him a priority through our upbringing. I had been living a clean, unobtrusive life where Samantha and I were comfortable and secure. We had our happy little apartment, Samantha had her school friends and I had my social life. Contentment had been taken for granted. But God had been unconsciously put on the sidelines. Then I met Rob and there started the disruption and transformation of our lives and my spiritual awareness.

I had been taken out of my comfort zone to something which, on the surface, seemed so much more exciting and fulfilling. I had fallen in love, but I had allowed my love to be wasted on a molten image, a delusion, a hollow dream. The surgery to my foot had been the turning point, the point at which the illusion had started to show signs of a false promise, and the dream of paradise on earth had been put in doubt. My dependence upon the flimsy security offered up by clinging to Rob had been a lesson in emotional survival. The discovery I had been played for a fool, was presented as part of that lesson. The unlikely events leading up to my meeting with Donovan online, and the tragic reality of nights Samantha and I had endured among the desperate people at the YMCA. It had all been God's plan at work. It all became so clear. I was now among people whose security was fragile at best and I was one of them, but I felt strength in my heart. I was going to become a part of the healing process, not only for myself and Samantha, but for hundreds of people. The depression of my soul, the grip of anxiety and hopelessness was being lifted from my heart and the sensation of excitement and happiness began to emerge. Samantha and I had been through hell, I would never fully know what long term psychological effect our ordeal would have on her, but her character was strong and she constantly gave me cause to swell with pride for the person she was turning out to be. I thanked God every day for this child.

We remained at Family Promise for nine months and as time went by I became more and more involved with their programmes of counseling. I was one of the lucky ones. I had a job and Samantha's school was nearby. I was able to save most of my wages and I was eventually in a position to look for a home Samantha and I could call our own.

The people at Family Promise, from Chip the chef who prepared take away packets of food for Samantha and I every morning, through to the administration staff, had been good to us in every possible way. When it came to finding our own home it almost felt as though that was what were leaving. At Family Promise the term Homeless loses its meaning. People find a home there and we were grateful for everything done for us. From the talks about depression and anxiety to other inmates and the exceptional meals Chip had prepared. We were leaving the stigma attached to "homeless people" but we would never truly leave Family Promise. The institution had become part of our lives and I had developed the confidence to be a powerful public speaker, something I did frequently at the various churches we attended and in contrast to the recurrent occasions I had contemplated taking my life, I now cherish it and give thanks to God for guiding us through the ordeals we had to suffer.

Epilogue

I HAVE ENDURED. I have suffered the humiliation of abuse and the loneliness of depression. I have seen the angel of death calling to me, calling me towards a dark hole from where there is no return and I have been tempted to answer the call.

I found God instead. I found a savior to whom I can turn, and a voice to express my confidence in the Lord Jesus Christ.

I have discovered the beauty of all things in God's creation and am grateful for his divine presence.

At thirty seven, a single mom living in the United States of America facing every day struggles, I have confidence God is taking care of me. I have no more fears, I am no longer weak, I am now whole. I am confident within myself and got to say praise God.

I found a calling in becoming a public speaker and every day I look forward to going out and encourage others to believe the God I serve can perform miracles if you believe.

Standing up on a public platform to speak in public was one of the hardest tasks I ever undertook. I never had the confidence but God covered for me and today I can testify I have been redeemed. I make time for the depressed person, I pray with and for them. I encourage the sick that God can be a doctor in the medical room and a lawyer in the court room. God is able to do anything and can move mountains just as he changed my life.

Today I live my life in the glory of God, honoring him daily for his divine intervention in my life. I have been gifted and God has called upon my voice to encourage others to live a life of happiness with Jesus as their guide.

I stand up in front of the world with absolute confidence, no stage fright or trepidation and share the word of God. I want the world to know that God loves us all and if we cast all our fears, troubles, and sorrows on him, trust in him he will deliver us from the horrors of our nightmares and misery.

I leave no space in my heart for hatred or revenge but will remove any obstacle trying to steal the joy I have found in God.

God wants us to be kind, be patient and love one another just as he has loved us. Share with others just as God has blessed and provide for us so should we for others. I take it upon myself to help others, anyone as long as I can, remembering how I have been helped by others through the words of God.

I thank God for giving me the strength and confidence to share my life and experiences in the hope others can draw inspiration from me.

THE END

Acknowledgments

I THANK GOD for everything he has done for me and continuing to do for me. I thank God for showing up for me when he did and letting me know what a friend I have in him. God stood with me when I thought there was no way; he fought my battles for me and strengthened me when I thought my life was over. God is the cure for depression and I want the world to know I am a survivor through Christ Jesus, through prayers I was able to break those demonic chains. I thank God for him being my strength. I thank God for all the pastors that prayed for me and with me, especially the one in England pastor Shadrack, Uwagboe he was powerful he made sure to call me every day and plead the blood upon me. He prayed with me and checked on me even if the time difference was five hours ahead, I will forever be grateful. I would like to thank Geleen Donavon for giving us a home to stay, where I found a form a stability and peace, met some lovely people who were so kind and loving at Family Promise, where my daughter and I stayed together and she wasn't taken away from me. I would like to thank my friend Donavon, Solomon for sticking with me through this all and helping me get my life back together and a job, for being a friend and a hero as well. I would like to thank my friend Rosemarie Montague for being a friend that loves me and encouraged me to do yoga, not forgetting my dear beloved friend Karl Turkle for staying on the phone with me when I checked in at the shelter, thank you to Chris Hall for giving me the idea I should write a book that will help others know God and get out of depression. Thanks to Sabina Augustine for calling me on the phone on March 25th when I was this close to committing suicide for this pressure was too much for my brain. I thank God for allowing her to make the time and encourage me that I was beautiful and even if I am black God sees me and hears me. I would like to thank my therapist Philip Baird for taking the time to allowing me to vent out my problems and helping me in finding a home, all the efforts that were put in it was appreciated. I would like to thank my cousins Anthony Descartes and Welton Egerton for helping me financially and kind words of encouragement. I'd like to thank Anthony Pagano and Ian Gosman for being a true friend supporting me financially at times. I would like to thank Alana Francis for being there for me all the way and still standing by myself. Thanks to all the prayers that were sent my way I really appreciated it very much and still do. Thank you to everyone who were a shoulder to lean on and was there for me when I needed a friend.

Edited by Ian Mackenzie. (A South African author)

If you have any questions, comments or need help please contact the author at Ingridcharlery74@gmail.com.

CPSIA information can be obtained
at www.ICGtesting.com
Printed in the USA
FFHW021629100419
51646398-57090FF